D1604196

Capital Campaigns

Everything You NEED to Know

Linda Lysakowski, ACFRE

Capital
Campaigns

Everything You NEED to Know

Capital Campaigns: Everything You NEED to Know
One of the **In the Trenches**™ series
Published by
CharityChannel Press, an imprint of CharityChannel LLC
30021 Tomas, Suite 300
Rancho Santa Margarita, CA 92688-2128 USA

http://charitychannel.com

ISBN: 978-0-9841580-6-5
Library of Congress Control Number: 2011936060

13 12 11 10 8 7 6 5 4 3 2 1

Printed in the United States of America

This and most CharityChannel Press books are available at special quantity discounts for bulk purchases for sales promotions, premiums, fundraising, or educational use. For information, contact CharityChannel Press, 30021 Tomas, Suite 300, Rancho Santa Margarita, CA 92688-2128 USA. +1 949-589-5938

About the Author

Linda Lysakowski, ACFRE

Linda is President/CEO of CAPITAL VENTURE, a full-service consulting firm with offices throughout the United States. Linda has managed capital campaigns ranging from $250,000 to over $30 million, helped dozens of nonprofit organizations achieve their development goals, and has trained more than 20,000 professionals in all aspects of development.

Linda is one of fewer than 100 professionals worldwide to hold the Advanced Certified Fund Raising Executive designation. She is a graduate of the Association of Fundraising Professionals (AFP) Faculty Training Academy and is a frequent presenter at regional and international conferences, including CharityChannel conferences and AFP conferences.

Linda is also a prolific writer. Her books include: *Recruiting and Training Fundraising Volunteers, The Development Plan,* and *Fundraising as a Career: What, Are You Crazy?* She is co-author of *The Essential Nonprofit Fundraising Handbook,* and co-editor and contributing author of *YOU and Your Nonprofit.* She is contributing author to *The Fundraising Feasibility Study—It's Not About the Money.*

Acknowledgements

I would like to thank all the clients and colleagues who have worked with me on capital campaigns throughout my career, starting with my first campaign experience as a staff member at Alvernia University. Special thanks go to Kathryn Short, who encouraged me to write this book and helped me organize the book. And, of course, my husband, Marty, who patiently and lovingly supports my writing career.

Contents

Foreword

The idea of raising a large amount of money in a finite period of time can be enormously attractive to many organizations and many people in a leadership role. The threshold of success for any capital campaign lies in preparation before, during and after this escalated fundraising effort. Linda's book is not only a "must read" for anyone embarking on a capital campaign, it is also a "must follow" because her chapters are beautifully organized in the logical fashion that make it easy to a take all the necessary steps for a successful capital campaign.

I particularly like Linda's emphasis that all the insights she reveals regarding capital campaign fundraising can be applied to every-day fundraising. So often we have the tendency to compartmentalize our fundraising methods when we are raising annual funds verses major gifts verses capital or endowment campaign funds. Linda's book gives you powerful learning tools for your prospective capital campaign as well as all your other fundraising areas.

Lastly I am personally thrilled that Linda included chapters on cultivating people for capital campaign gifts, making the ASK, then stewarding each gift. Often these essential elements are taken for granted or they get lost to seemingly more important issues of the campaign budget, marketing materials, and naming opportunities.

This book is truly a compilation of Linda's talents as an extremely accomplished fundraising professional. I highly recommend you read each and every part regardless if you are starting a campaign or are in an existing campaign. There are some real jewels here you will not want to miss!

Laura Fredricks
International Philanthropic Advisor
Author: *The ASK: How to Ask for your Nonprofit Cause, Creative Project, or Business Venture*

Introduction

After more than twenty years in the field of philanthropy and working with capital campaigns ranging in size from less than $200,000 to more than $30 million, I've seen a lot of commonalities in campaigns, no matter what the size, the type of organization, or the purpose of the campaign.

While there are many factors that can affect the outcome of a campaign, I have noted that campaigns are always more successful if the organization has the following in place: The organization is better prepared internally to run a campaign, the community responds well to the case for support, and the organization is able to recruit top-notch campaign volunteers.

My goals in writing this book are to help organizations of all sizes learn how to assess readiness for a campaign, how to better prepare for a capital campaign, and how to organize their campaigns effectively.

Another important goal is to help development staff and other nonprofit leaders stop dreading the very words, "capital campaign." My goal is that you will come to realize that a well-run campaign not only helps your organization achieve its immediate goal of a new building, a renovated building or a strong program endowment. The ultimate result of a well-run capital campaign is that your organization is much stronger going forward. A successful campaign will help your organization increase its annual giving program, develop or strengthen a planned giving program, and, most importantly, advance its mission because of your successful fundraising program.

In this book you will learn first what a capital campaign is and how it is both different from and similar to other fundraising efforts with which you may be more familiar.

I will talk about the case for support and how it is developed and tested, usually through the planning study. The case should outline the organization's mission, vision, history, programs, community need, and how the project will fill this need. The case should present both emotional and rational reason for people to give to the campaign and provide various opportunities for participating in the campaign.

The role of the board of directors in a capital campaign is critical and is discussed in this book. The staff role is equally important in a campaign. Often staff members are overly involved in running special events, writing grant proposals, public relations activities, and sometimes even assuming program responsibilities. Therefore, I will address the importance of board involvement and how to manage a campaign even in a short-staffed organization.

It has long been my contention that volunteers are the key to a campaign's success. Volunteer involvement shows the community that you have public support for your organization. In this book, I will discuss the role of volunteers, how to find the right volunteers, and how to recruit and retain volunteers.

Of course, major donors are needed in any campaign, no matter what the dollar goal of the campaign, and in this book you will learn how to identify, cultivate, and solicit donors.

We will also talk about the planning study process and how it can help you prepare for a successful campaign.

You will learn how to organize your campaign—everything from the campaign plan and budget, campaign events and publicity, to organizing volunteers and recognizing donors.

Finally, we talk about "life after the campaign." I have found that one of the best parts about a capital campaign is the fact that a successful campaign can only serve to strengthen ongoing fundraising efforts, so the final chapter in this book will tell you how to build on your success to make your development program even better going forward.

In this book you will find many tools and forms to help you plan your campaign. Throughout each chapter you will find sidebars with definitions, important facts, and tips to make special note of when planning your campaign.

So, read on, and let me know if this book helped you understand the process of a capital campaign and, most of all, if you moved from a total dread of the very word, "campaign," or even from a moderate comfort level with capital campaigning to true enthusiasm for the campaign.

Chapter One

What is a Capital Campaign?

···→ What is a capital campaign and what is different about it?

···→ What are the keys to a successful campaign?

···→ How do I know if my organization is ready for a campaign?

While virtually all nonprofits need to raise money on an ongoing basis for operating expenses, the *capital campaign* is unique in several ways. It is different in purpose since the money is used to offset major capital expenses: building construction or renovation, major equipment purchases, building an endowment for the future, and/ or program expansion. The campaign is also different for many smaller organizations, because it is a once-in-a-lifetime experience that may be the largest amount of money your organization has attempted to raise.

Before we address the differences, however, I would like to talk about the similarities between capital campaigns and your annual fundraising efforts. Although we often think of the mystique that surrounds capital campaigns as something totally unique and mysterious, there are many principles of capital campaigns that can easily be applied to your annual fundraising efforts. There is an important reason I discuss the similarities first: Even if, after reading this book, you decide you do not need or are not ready for a capital campaign, I hope you will take the lessons learned in this book and apply them to all your fundraising efforts.

Some of the similarities that you should note are the importance of a compelling case for support, the fact that board support is critical, and the difference that volunteers can make in your fundraising efforts. The infrastructure built in preparation for a capital campaign is the foundation for a strong fundraising program, so even if you don't move forward with a campaign, you should build this strong

---

The Keys to Success

Many of the principles of capital campaigning can also be translated into other fundraising activities, and these include the keys to a successful campaign.

◆ There must be a compelling case for support;

◆ The board of directors must fully support the campaign;

◆ A strong infrastructure must be in place;

◆ Volunteer involvement is critical.

 practical tip

---

infrastructure. One of the key concepts of capital campaigns is that they only succeed if you work from the top down and from the inside out. This means that you start your campaign by seeking the leadership gifts first and by making sure that the board and staff are the first groups to make their pledges. Both of these concepts can also be extremely helpful in your annual giving efforts. Conducting your board and staff appeal before approaching others for annual giving will show that your "family" supports your organization. Planning your major gift calls first and securing some lead gifts to your annual campaign will help others to jump on board because they feel your annual appeal, like your capital campaign, has a good chance to succeed. Another key capital campaign principle is that the campaign must first be won on paper before it can be won in reality. This principle stresses the importance of having a detailed and well-thought-out plan for your capital campaign, as well as for your annual giving program. Sounds like a lot of similarities, right? So what makes a campaign different from your other fundraising efforts?

One primary difference that distinguishes capital campaigns from other fundraising programs is that there is a specified time frame for raising the money; it is not an ongoing activity like your annual fund. Another major difference is that the capital campaign is a far more public activity than most of your organization's fundraising efforts. Another major difference that is often overlooked is the way donors think about a capital campaign— they usually make donations to capital campaigns from assets rather than their disposable income from which they make most annual fund contributions.

Usually the capital campaign is used to raise significant sums of money to acquire or renovate a building, but often the campaign's focus is on building an endowment for the future. In some cases, campaigns are initiated to fund extraordinary expenditures of a capital nature, such as an expensive piece of equipment for a hospital or a new fire truck for a fire company.

For many people, the emphasis in a capital campaign may be on the "pain." Campaigns do tend to disrupt the routine of the development office and the entire organization might feel the strain of the extra effort required

A **capital campaign** is an intense effort on the part of a nonprofit organization to raise significant dollars in a specified period of time.

for a year, two years, or more, depending on the size of the campaign. However, campaigns have several great benefits, which for many organizations offset the work involved. Some of these include:

◆ *Raising the money to fund a one-time need for the organization.* In most cases having a building that meets the needs of the community served by the organization.

◆ *Strengthening the organization's infrastructure.* Working on a campaign requires that your organization evaluate its readiness for a campaign, and subsequently build an infrastructure to run a campaign, including staffing, board commitment, software to manage the campaign, gift acceptance polices, etc. This stronger infrastructure will leave your organization in a much better position to raise funds on an ongoing basis.

> In cases where a capital campaign is for a new building or expansion of an existing facility, consideration should always be given to adding an endowment portion to the campaign goal. Remember that a larger facility will almost always involve increased operating expenses. It is also important to remember that the focus of the campaign should not be on the building or amassing a large endowment fund, but on the benefits to the community that this facility or endowment will provide through expanded, increased or more efficient programming.

important

◆ *Volunteer involvement.* Most campaigns are very volunteer intensive often involving hundreds of volunteers in the organization's vision. A good campaign organization will include a post-campaign plan for retaining the involvement of volunteers.

◆ *Increased public awareness.* During a campaign, there will be great deal of publicity and cultivation efforts to help raise awareness of the organization in the community. These efforts, as with the strengthened infrastructure, will help the organization's future fundraising efforts.

The first things you need to determine are whether you need a campaign, how much money you need to raise, and whether your organization is ready for a campaign.

Any discussion of a capital campaign should start with the strategic planning process. Your board and staff must together evaluate your organization's needs for programs and services, and in the planning process should ask questions such as:

❑ What is the potential for growth in our organization?

❑ How are the demographics of our constituents changing?

❑ Are we prepared to meet the needs of our community?

❑ Is our facility adequate to handle growing needs and if not, what do we need to do to improve our facilities?

Generally this discussion is part of your strategic planning process and, if your organization does not have a strategic plan in place, this should be your first step. Even before engaging a consultant to conduct a planning study for the campaign, you should engage a facilitator to lead you through the strategic planning process. Many organizations plan a day-long retreat with board and staff, facilitated by a capital campaign consultant to lead them through this process. At this point, often an architect or construction manager is brought in to help you determine how your facilities need to change in order to fulfill your mission. The campaign consultant can help you figure out a timeline for the campaign to coordinate with the construction timeline. It is wise to involve these experts from the very beginning to save you from heading off in a direction that is not feasible.

Your finance committee then needs to look at how your organization can finance these needs. They should address questions such as:

❑ Will the added programs you can provide in the new facility bring in more revenue and what costs are associated with adding programs?

❑ Do you need a short-term loan to fund the early stages of construction?

❑ How much does your organization have in reserves that could be applied to construction costs?

❑ How much do you think you can raise from the community in a capital campaign? This figure will be confirmed during the planning study, but it is good to have a preliminary campaign goal in mind before you engage a consultant for the study.

Once you reach consensus that a campaign is in order, a steering committee is then appointed to take the organization to the next step. This group is not the campaign cabinet, but rather a small group of people who are close to the organization and will be engaged in the preliminary planning process. Members of this steering committee usually include those with experience in construction, finance, and fundraising. Both board and staff members generally serve on the steering committee. Most organizations include on this committee:

❑ The chief executive officer of the organization

❑ The chief development officer

❑ The board chair or a designee of the chair who will be heavily involved in the campaign

❑ The facilities chair and/or staff person in charge of facilities

❑ The chair of the finance committee of the board

❑ The chief financial officer of the organization

❑ The chair of the development committee of the board

❑ A major donor (if you have identified someone who is thought to be a lead donor and/or key volunteer for the campaign)

"Are You Ready for a Capital Campaign?" Evaluation Worksheet

Circle a number for each statement:
0 = Serious problem exists, 5 = Goal completed

❑ Our organization meets all legal/ethical requirements to engage in fundraising activities.	0 1 2 3 4 5
❑ Our organization has a solid infrastructure.	0 1 2 3 4 5
❑ Our organization is financially stable.	0 1 2 3 4 5
❑ Our board president/chair is recognized as a strong, able community leader.	0 1 2 3 4 5

❏ Our board has good structure and is functioning well.	0 1 2 3 4 5
❏ Our board has reached consensus on the campaign plan and goal.	0 1 2 3 4 5
❏ Our board is willing to work on the campaign.	0 1 2 3 4 5
❏ Our CEO is a leader who will help promote the campaign.	0 1 2 3 4 5
❏ Our CEO is experienced and respected in the community.	0 1 2 3 4 5
❏ Our staff has enough experience and knowledge in the field of fundraising.	0 1 2 3 4 5
❏ Our staff has enough time to work on the campaign.	0 1 2 3 4 5
❏ A long-range plan with written goals is in place.	0 1 2 3 4 5
❏ A strong development program is in place.	0 1 2 3 4 5
❏ A marketing and publicity plan is in place.	0 1 2 3 4 5
❏ Our organization serves a real need in the community.	0 1 2 3 4 5
❏ The consumers of our organization think highly of our programs.	0 1 2 3 4 5
❏ Our organization has a high public image.	0 1 2 3 4 5
❏ There are individuals who could give 10 percent of the campaign goal if they desire to do so.	0 1 2 3 4 5
❏ Our top 100 donors have been identified and cultivated.	0 1 2 3 4 5
❏ Our campaign initiative is innovative, exciting, ambitious, and worthy of support.	0 1 2 3 4 5

For the expanded version of this *"Are Your Ready for a Capital Campaign?" Evaluation Worksheet,* contact the author at:

 http://charitychannel.com/cc/linda-lysakowski

To Recap

A capital campaign is usually recommended when you need to raise a large sum of money in a limited timeframe for bricks and mortar needs, endowment, or a special project or piece of high-ticket equipment.

The keys to a successful campaign are having your infrastructure in order, making sure your board is committed to the project, being able to make a compelling case for support and involving a significant number of community volunteers in addition to board and staff.

Capital campaign planning should start with overall organization-wide strategic planning in order to assure that the campaign is indeed needed to better serve your community. Once the board is in agreement that a campaign is a possibility, a steering committee should be appointed to begin the early planning for the campaign.

Many of the principles of a capital campaign can easily be applied to your annual giving program and a capital campaign will help strengthen your organization for all its future fundraising efforts.

Chapter Two

Are You Ready for a Campaign— Infrastructure?

IN THIS CHAPTER

···➔ How important is it that we have a development staff person to run a campaign?

···➔ What policies and procedures do we need in the development office in order to be prepared for a campaign?

···➔ What type of donor software do we need to help manage campaign data?

Once your board has reached consensus on the campaign and appointed a steering committee, the next step is to do an internal assessment of your organization's readiness for a campaign. Often this is done through a formal development audit process. If time or circumstances do not permit a full-blown audit, the consultant chosen to do the study should perform an internal assessment as part of the planning study. In either case the consultant will be looking at various aspects of the organization's infrastructure.

Infrastructure includes the staffing of your organization as well as your office systems and procedures, including software, gift acceptance policies and office procedures. Managing a capital campaign will be challenging if your organization does not have its house in order.

Your staff must recognize that everyone in the organization, from the CEO on down must be involved in the campaign, with the chief development officer playing the major role of managing the campaign, working with the campaign consultant, board, and volunteers to assure success. CEOs may spend up to 50-75 percent of their time on campaign activities such as cultivating and soliciting donors and attending campaign meetings and events. The chief executive of your organization plays an important role in identifying, cultivating, and soliciting major donors and should be visible at campaign events. Many major donors will want to talk to the person in charge of the organization. The leader of the organization can often convey the vision better than anyone else. Corporate and foundation CEOs will usually want to meet with the CEO, whom they think about as a peer. A visionary leader can inspire donors and volunteers. If the chief executive of your organization is absent from important major gift calls and key campaign events, volunteers will lose faith in the commitment of your organization to this campaign and donors will feel that they are not considered important enough for a visit by the CEO.

Staffing for a campaign is critical. No matter what the size of the organization and the development staff, consideration must be given to the amount of time the campaign will take from the staff's time. This is an especially sensitive area for organizations that do not have a formal development office. In many smaller organizations, the executive director wears the development hat along with all the other duties of the key staff person. The executive director of your organization, even if you have a development office, will most likely spend a great deal time on the campaign once it gets up and running. If the executive director is not prepared to accept this role, the campaign will suffer from this lack of commitment. Leadership-level donors will want to talk with the CEO of the organization before making a major commitment. Donor cultivation is another key role of the CEO, so there will be countless meetings, lunches, cocktail parties, and early-morning breakfasts at which the CEO will play a leading role.

The development office will coordinate all these cultivation events, working closely with the campaign consultant. In addition the development office will be responsible for prospect research, organizing volunteers, assuring proper stewardship, etc. For many small organizations, the chief development function may revolve around special events, which are very time consuming for staff. If the organization is focused on special events that may be bringing in modest revenues, instead of channeling the required amount of time and energy into the capital campaign, the campaign will suffer.

As we will discuss in future chapters, although the role of volunteers and consultants is important in a campaign, the staff role should not be under-emphasized. In cases where there is no development office, often a campaign director will be hired or a staff person might be pulled from current duties to manage the campaign.

A word of caution when there is no development director in place—there must be someone who will be assigned full time to campaign coordination. This is not a task that can be done in a staff member's "spare time." Volunteers and donors need to know there is a person responsible for managing all the aspects of the campaign and someone they can go to with questions. Stewardship is a crucial part of all fundraising and is particularly important in a capital campaign.

important

Other areas of infrastructure that need to be addressed are policies and procedures, technology, and overall strength of the organization. It will be crucial to have a software system that can manage campaign data, and to have gift acceptance policies in place regarding what type of gifts you will accept, from whom you will accept gifts, policies for naming opportunities within the campaign, and how you will manage and/or dispose of non-cash gifts.

One of the things that will make campaign management and stewardship flow more efficiently is a good campaign software package. You will need to access past giving history of donors and be able to use this donor history, combined with additional research, to qualify prospective donors and assign them to an appropriate solicitor. Donor history is an invaluable resource in the preparation for a capital campaign since, in most cases, the major gifts in a campaign will come from those who are already supporting the organization.

In preparing for a campaign, you will need to have specific fundraising software in place that allows for campaign coding structure, recording multi-year pledges, and generating campaign reports. The coding of the software system is essential to be able to sort prospects by the division in which they will be contacted (i.e. leadership gifts, major gifts, etc.) and to assign a solicitor to every prospect, enabling the campaign director to sort prospect names by solicitor in order to track the success of volunteer solicitors.

Another important function of the chosen software system will be to generate the campaign reports that will be needed for the board, the campaign cabinet and committees, and lending institutions. For example, your board will want to track pledges received and cash received against those pledges; the campaign cabinet and various committees will need to see overall campaign progress reports and reports within their division by solicitor. If you are seeking interim financing to cover the construction costs while pledges are being paid, your lending institution will want to see a cash flow projection showing how many pledges are outstanding and when it is anticipated those pledges will be paid.

Sometimes organizations feel they can do all this by customizing a program like Microsoft Access or Excel; however, it is often "penny wise and pound foolish" to resist purchasing software designed especially for fundraising and which will provide all the tools necessary to manage a campaign, with little or no customization. Purchasing fundraising software provides you with added benefits of having support from the software company, manuals explaining the various functions of the software, and a group of users who are operating the same system and can provide an additional means of support for you and your staff. It is important to have a designated database manager in

For a list of software companies, contact the author at:

 http://charitychannel.com/cc/linda-lysakowski

 practical tip

place who can devote the time needed to manage the campaign aspects of the development program, and that this person receive the training and support necessary to assure accurate data entry and reporting.

In addition to staffing and software, internal policies and procedures are another essential ingredient that must be assessed. You need to have gift acceptance policies in place that will provide staff and volunteers with guidelines for what type of gifts will be accepted during the campaign, from whom gifts will be accepted, how these gifts will be recognized and, in some cases, how they will be disposed of. Gift acceptance policies should be in place for every nonprofit but they will be especially important during a capital campaign when you are seeking major gifts and might be offered unusual gifts, such as gifts of real estate, artwork, building materials, etc. Also in the capital campaign, you will be dealing with named giving opportunities and you will need to establish policies regarding the size of donations required to name after the donor a building or areas of a building. Also, if your campaign involves endowment funds, you will need policies regarding types of gifts you will accept, how endowment funds will be invested, and how they will be spent.

Internal procedures should also be in place for accepting, recording and acknowledging pledges and gifts received. For instance, procedures

---

Some examples of things that should be included in your gift acceptance policies are:

◆ From whom will we accept/not accept gifts?

◆ How will gifts of stock be accepted and invested or disposed of?

◆ How will gifts be recognized?

◆ How will excess funds be invested while the project is being completed?

◆ How will non-cash gifts such as real estate, art work, etc. be appraised, accepted and used or disposed of?

◆ What types of gifts-in-kind will be accepted and counted towards the campaign?

◆ How will gifts of life insurance and other planned gifts be handled and counted in the campaign?

important

In **Appendix E,** you will find a Campaign Assignments Worksheet to help you determine what skills and talents you have in-house and for which services you might need to engage outside help.

practical tip

should cover who opens mail, photocopies checks, makes the bank deposit, and signs the acknowledgement letters? These procedures should be in place for all fundraising but will be especially important in the campaign since this might be the first time you accept multi-year pledges in addition to one-time gifts. You will need to determine who signs the thank you letters—the volunteer involved in making the ask, staff, or board member. You should also determine how to code capital campaign gifts in your software system in order to assure donations are designated for the campaign and that pledges are recorded accurately so you can generate cash flow reports. Coding volunteer activity is especially important during the campaign. You will also be dealing with a lot of major gifts, that might require special treatment, such as notifying the volunteers involved in the solicitation of the gifts when pledges are received.

To Recap

Staff must commit the time necessary to plan and manage the campaign. The CEO will play a major role in identifying, cultivating, and soliciting donors. If there is no development staff person, you'll need to assign someone to manage the campaign. The charts in **Appendix E** can help you assess what skills and talents you have internally and which ones you might need to hire staff or engage consultant to help with.

The development office needs policies and procedures in place before soliciting donors during the campaign. A donor database software package is needed to allow you to manage data, acknowledge donors and prepare campaign reports. Gift acceptance policies and office procedures are especially important during a campaign.

Chapter Three

Are You Ready for a Campaign—Who Else Needs to Be Involved Besides Staff?

IN THIS CHAPTER

- ··➔ What role will my board play in the campaign?

- ··➔ What happens if the board is not fully supportive of the campaign?

- ··➔ Do we need a consultant to help us run a campaign?

- ··➔ Where do we find donors for our campaign?

- ··➔ How do we get volunteers to help?

W e've talked about the infrastructure needed to run a capital campaign. Human resources, in addition to staff, are the next topics to address. Who needs to be involved in the campaign, other than staff? There are several areas to consider in this regard—the board's commitment, volunteer leadership, working with consultants, and finding a pool of donors for the campaign.

The Board's Role

The board should first endorse the campaign by issuing a board resolution to proceed with a campaign. Every board member must contribute financially to the campaign at a meaningful level (which is different for each board member) before you ask others to contribute. There should also be a number of board members who agree to serve on the capital campaign cabinet. And, every board member should be somehow involved in the campaign—asking others to give, serving on various committees, identifying and cultivating potential donors, publicly endorsing, and promoting the campaign.

Board commitment is one of the key areas that need to be addressed before moving forward with a campaign. Has the board reached consensus that this campaign is necessary and has the board agreed on a preliminary goal for the campaign? Do board members understand their role in the campaign and that their role will include a financial commitment as well as working on the campaign? I recommend that, once your board has decided a campaign is in order, they pass a formal resolution at a board meeting to proceed with planning a campaign. It is wise at this juncture in the planning process to invite a consultant to talk to your board members about their role in the campaign, so they understand what is involved in running a campaign before they pass a resolution to move forward. Once the planning study begins, you will need board input into the preliminary case for support and the development of an interviewee list. Although you shouldn't have a case statement "written by committee," the board should at the very least be aware of what will be sent out to community members who will be interviewed. Members of the board serving on the steering committee are generally the ones responsible for approving the preliminary case statement. All board members should be invited to review and add names to the list of potential interviewees. Staff and the consultant generally prepare a preliminary list of interviewees and review it with the board in order to finalize and prioritize the list. At least some, if not all, board members will be interviewed during the study. And, assuming the study is positive and the campaign moves ahead, board members need to understand that 100 percent of them must give to the campaign before asking the public to support the campaign.

Depending on the size of your board, between three and nine members—maybe even more if the board is larger than twenty people—should also be committed to working on the campaign cabinet and recruiting others to become involved. All board members must be willing to support the campaign to the extent they can contribute both time and dollars. Some ways board members can support the campaign include:

◆ Making a personal financial commitment

◆ Seeking gifts from their employers or people with whom they do business

◆ Opening the door to potential donors

◆ Making presentations to prospective donors, either individually or in a group setting

◆ Promoting the campaign within their circles of influence

◆ Attending campaign meetings and events

The presence of board members at key campaign events will be required in order to show united support of the project. Lack of board support will be negatively perceived by the community of prospective and current donors who attend these events, and can be the kiss of death to your campaign.

It will be helpful, although not always necessary, that at least some of your board members have the ability to make a substantial leadership gift to the campaign. Board members should be expected to make a "stretch gift" to the campaign. They are, after all, the ones who will set the pace for others. If possible, a board member should be approached to make the lead gift to and possibly chair the campaign. The chair should always be someone who has made a significant gift to the campaign, so that person can set the example and ask others to make gifts at a similar level. It is, however, unreasonable to expect that *every* board has the ability to attract a major donor. This depends very much on the makeup of the board, which is why many organizations preparing for a campaign start to beef up their boards in advance of the campaign. Your organization might be one whose board is not made up of people with affluence and influence.

> Volunteer leadership is the single most important element of a successful campaign.
>
> **principle**

But do not be discouraged. For grass roots organizations and those with community-based boards, the lack of cash and clout on the board can be compensated for with the right approach to recruiting key volunteer leadership.

Involving Volunteers

The board and staff alone should not try to run a campaign without support of key community leaders. If you do not involve community leaders in the campaign, it is unlikely your organization will receive broad financial support from the community. Donors want to see that people they know and respect support the campaign. The board, itself, will not have as many contacts in the community as will be available through building a strong volunteer leadership structure. This is especially important if your board is small or weak. If you don't involve those in your community who are known as philanthropic and well connected, it will be difficult to reach philanthropists, major corporations, and foundations, or even government support. However, it is also important to make sure your volunteers are committed to the mission of your organization.

Before recruiting people to serve on the campaign cabinet, the steering committee should review a list of potential donors and try to invite those who have the greatest giving potential to become involved in the campaign. The list of corporate and individual donors developed through the planning study process can serve as the basis for recruiting campaign leadership. It will be vital to include key community leaders in the planning study process. It is much easier to invite these leaders to serve in a campaign capacity if they've been included in the planning process.

Volunteers will also be able to expand the scope of your prospect base and will be far more effective at soliciting their peers than anyone within the organization on their own. The volunteer might, in fact, be the only person who can open the door to a major donor.

What will the volunteers do and how many do you need? You may need hundreds of volunteers to run a capital campaign. Although this may sound a bit scary, it can be easily done by using the recruitment steps found in Chapter Seven. We talk more about developing position descriptions and recruiting volunteers in that chapter. But for now remember that the importance of volunteers must be understood by the board, staff, and steering committee. Starting with the campaign leadership, it will be important to find the right person to do the right job. Some volunteers will be needed for planning campaign events and coordinating campaign publicity, but the majority of campaign volunteers will be involved in the important tasks of identifying, cultivating, and soliciting donors. It is critical to have an organization chart and position description for every volunteer job within the campaign.

Handle volunteer recruitment with extreme care. Organizations often want to jump the gun and start recruiting campaign leadership before they have a clear idea of the expectations for these volunteers. It is vital to have a campaign plan in place that includes, among other things, position descriptions for all volunteer roles and timelines for each committee.

important

How do you find volunteers? The planning study report is the first place to look for potential volunteers. Also, ask board members, other volunteers and staff for their suggestions about people who can help. And, of course, most campaign volunteers will be inviting other volunteers to join their committee or somehow get involved.

Trying to fit volunteers into roles after they are recruited is like hiring a staff person and then deciding what the organization wants the person to do. The volunteer recruitment process must be handled just as carefully as one would handle hiring a staff person—with due diligence and thoughtfulness of the best role for this volunteer.

Do You Need a Consultant?

Most organizations hire a consultant when considering a campaign because they don't have the time, expertise, or knowledge to run a campaign on their own. You need to understand what a consultant can and cannot do for you. Consultants do not raise the money for you. They are like the coach on the football team, and the volunteers are the players who will actually make the asks. So if you think the consultant is the magic bullet you need to land those big gifts, this might not be the case. Think about how you would feel if a consultant you did not know came to you and asked for a gift. Wouldn't you respond better to someone in your community you know and respect and who is giving at a level they are asking you to contribute? However, there are many things a consultant can do to help you with your campaign. Hiring a consultant is never a guarantee that your campaign will succeed. But the objectivity, creativity, knowledge, and expertise a consultant can bring to the campaign can get you started off on the right foot. If your budget is limited, you should hire a consultant early in the process to do your study and prepare a campaign plan. The consultant may be able to tell you how you can manage a campaign on your own or with limited consulting help, once a solid plan is in place.

Here are some resources to help find the right consultant for your organization:

◆ charitychannel.com

◆ www.npocentral.org

◆ www.afpnet.org

◆ www.nonprofitnationalresourcedirectory.com

 practical tip

Finding the Right Consultant

Consultants can offer many areas of expertise in different areas of fundraising. There are grant writing consultants, planned giving consultants, event consultants, search firms, capital campaign consultants, board development consultants, and consultants who can help you develop a plan or audit your organization's development office. Some full service firms offer a combination of or all of these services. But, you need to know what type of consultant you are looking for. Do not hire a grant writer to run a capital campaign; make sure the firms you talk to have experience in running capital campaigns.

Where do you begin your search for a consultant? You can start by asking other nonprofits in your community that have held campaigns about their experiences. However, a consultant that did a good job for one organization might not be right for yours. You can also check out sources such as CharityChannel's Consultants Registry Online, the Association of Fundraising Professionals' Consultant Directory, and other resources listed in this chapter. If your state has a statewide association of nonprofits, many offer consultant listings, as well. And, of course, the Internet is a good place to start. Before we talk about what you do after you've identified several firms you think would be appropriate for your campaign, let's talk about consultant fees.

Have you budgeted adequately for consultant fees?

You need to understand that you are not usually paying the consultant for the hours they work, but you are paying for their knowledge, their experience, and their expertise. Often, board members who have not worked with consultants before are not prepared to pay the fees involved, because they do not understand this concept. Also, be aware of other costs, such as travel expenses if you are hiring a consultant outside the area. Ask what type of hotel accommodations they expect, what typical airfares will run, do they charge for mileage, phone calls, faxes, etc. Is there a charge for materials they provide? It is best to seek several proposals and compare fees, but make sure to compare apples to apples. One consultant might charge extra for travel costs, and another might include them in the overall monthly fee. Ask if there are hidden costs such as telephone, postage, etc. Also remember that the consultant with the lowest fee might not always be the best option. There are many other things to consider such as the consultant's experience, chemistry with your staff and board, and the availability of the consultant's time. Be very cautious about a consultant who offers to do a study for an extremely low fee, because you may not get an unbiased study if the consultant is pricing the study low in order to "land the campaign contract."

What are the criteria you are looking for in a consultant?

Some organizations feel it is important to have a local consultant; others look for someone with a national reputation and experience. Some organizations feel it is important to hire someone who has worked with similar organizations; for example a YMCA may want someone who has worked with other YMCAs. If the consultant is truly knowledgeable about their work, these things are often not as important as they seem. Some important criteria to look for are: Does the consultant seem to understand your needs? Do you feel the chemistry between the staff and board is good? Is the consultant willing to learn enough about your organization and your constituents to effectively help you present your case? And, of course, ask about their approach to capital campaigns and what services they provide.

Ask about the consultant's work style. Will they provide actual work products, or are they providing you with direction so you can produce the products yourself? Will they be on site, or do they work from their own office? How accessible is the consultant to you by email? Make sure the style they offer is what your organization needs. Does their personality fit your organization's culture? Some organizations want a polished, sophisticated person, while others may prefer a more down-to-earth style. You need to be comfortable with your consultant's style.

The RFP

Many organizations prepare an RFP, or Request for Proposal, and distribute it to the firms they want to consider for their campaign. You should be aware that some consultants do not respond to RFPs, because they get most of their work through word-of-mouth referrals, or because they feel the RFP process is too impersonal. If you are going to send out an RFP, it should not be too lengthy. Many consultants shy away from an RFP that looks like a government proposal. (I once had to sign a contract to conduct a planning that stated I would not be using any hazardous materials— this was for a state-run university. I can laugh about it now, but I almost did not apply for the job because its RFP was so restrictive and obviously written to cover all contingencies from the university's landscapers to major construction projects, but it was hardly suitable for accounting firms and fundraising consultants.) If you do not issue a formal RFP, you should at the very least supply the firms you are considering with some basic information about your proposed campaign, such as:

❑ The projected amount of your campaign goal.

❑ The purpose of the campaign, i.e. building, endowment, equipment.

❑ If you want a proposal just for the planning study or for the study and the campaign itself.

❑ Your expected timeframe for the campaign, as well as the due date for the proposal and your anticipated decision date.

❑ Basic information about your organization such as your mission, vision, budget size, list of board members, and annual giving history.

The Interviews

You will most likely want to meet in person with several firms before making a decision. This will give you the opportunity to observe the consultant's style and assess the chemistry between the consultant and your staff and board. Most organizations plan these interviews with the steering committee rather than with the entire board, followed by the steering committee's recommendations to the board about which firm to hire. It is usually too difficult to get the entire board together for hours at a time to conduct interviews. Schedule the interviews far enough in advance to assure that the consultants have time to adequately prepare and arrange their schedules, particularly if there is travel involved.

Once you've scheduled the interviews, allow enough time for each firm to make an effective presentation. Usually about an hour for each firm is sufficient. Be sure to have a "timekeeper" track the time used by each firm if you have others waiting for their turn. Most committees cannot interview more than three or four firms in one day. It is wise to also leave time between interviews so that the committee can discuss their impressions about each firm before the next group comes in. You might even prepare a "score sheet"

> Remember consultants do not raise money for you, they help your staff and volunteers develop the skills and relationships to raise the money.

principle

for committee members to rank each firm, and then review these scores when the interviews are completed. One question you should always ask in the interview process is whether the interviewee is the person you will be working with. Some larger firms have sales representatives who may not necessarily be the consultant you would work with if you hire that firm.

References, Ethics and the Law

Be sure to ask for references from other clients the consultant has worked with. And ask if the consultant is a member of the Association of Fundraising Professionals (AFP) or another association that carries a standard of ethics. Also, many states require a consultants to register, so if your state is one of those, be sure that the consultant is registered.

The written contract

Always have a written contract or letter of agreement signed by your organization and the consultant. This contract should outline fees and other expenses, a schedule of when fees will be paid, a scope of work to be performed, a starting and ending date for the work, and a provision to extend or cancel the contract. If your state is one that requires consultant to register, they will also be required to file the contract with the regulatory authority and receive approval before they can begin work on the campaign.

Welcome the consultant into your organization

Once you've decided on a consultant, notify the other firms you considered of the decision, but only after you've notified the successful candidate. You should invite the consultant to a preliminary meeting to get the contracts signed, and introduce them to your organization's staff and board members who were not in the interview meetings. Be sure that the staff members of your organization who will be working with this consultant get to meet the consultant and know what is expected of them and of the consultant. A tour of your facility so that the consultant can get to meet program staff and others will be helpful. And, feel free to tell the consultant if you are unhappy or uncomfortable with anything they're doing.

The following checklist can help you find the right consultant for your campaign, or other institutional needs.

Selecting-a-Consultant Checklist

❑ Determine whether you need outside help—identify the problem, and achieve board/staff consensus that a consultant is needed.

❑ Select the appropriate type of consultant—Understand the specific type of services needed and types of professionals that are available, and determine budget.

❑ Identify possible consultants—Ask for referrals from colleagues and professional organizations.

❑ Make initial contact with possible consultants—Call, make notes of initial reaction, verify availability, and narrow the list to a few firms.

❑ Provide information about your organization—Ask what information they need, and determine if the timeline you've developed works for the consultant.

❑ Design interviews with consultants—Determine who in your organization will make the final hiring decision, how many firms will you interview, how much time will you allow for each interview, who will be involved, and what questions to ask.

❑ Conduct initial phone interviews—Assess consultant's understanding of your organization's needs, determine if their style and personality will fit your organization, obtain information on fees and expenses, ask for references, and request a written proposal.

❑ Receive and review proposals—Determine if the proposals meet your guidelines, check references, determine importance of personality, experience, approach and costs, and select finalists.

❑ Have finalists make presentation to board, committee and/or executive staff—Provide interviewers with information beforehand, guide discussion to pertinent questions, assess consultant's ability to command board/staff's interest, attention, and respect.

❑ Make decision—Inform the firm that is your final choice, set up meeting to negotiate contract.

❑ Don't notify your second, third, or fourth choices until your contract is signed, in case your first choice consultant is not available or contract negotiations fail.

❑ Welcome consultant to your organization and introduce them to key staff with whom they will be working.

Donors

Finally, there is one more group of people to evaluate and include in your plan—donors! That sounds pretty basic, that you need donors before entering into a campaign. But surprisingly many people feel that the campaign will generate its own interest in the organization and that you need to go out and find a whole cadre of new donors. While it is true that campaigns often do help you uncover and involve new donors, the majority of donors to your campaign will come from those who are already aware of and support your organization. So a careful study should be undertaken of the potential for major gifts among your organization's current donor pool.

One good way to evaluate giving potential is to look at the level of giving from past donors. Who is among the top 10 percent of your donors? Who are the loyal donors who give year after year, even if not at a significant level? Here is where the donor software discussed earlier comes in. If you have a good software system with up-to-date information, you will much more easily be able to develop a list of potential donors than if you need to search through hard copy records or rely on institutional memory. Although the planning study may uncover a whole new list of potential donors, the consultant will need a base of people to interview. So you should start preparing a list of potential donors as soon as you feel you are ready to start a planning study. We will cover the process of identifying, cultivating, and soliciting donors in future chapters, but don't forget to include any prospective leadership donors in your planning process.

To Recap

The role of the board is critical in a capital campaign. Every board member must make a personal financial commitment to the campaign, and each board member should be willing to assume some role in the campaign.

Volunteer leadership can make or break your campaign. Be sure to select the right chairperson(s) and to develop job descriptions for all the volunteers who will be involved in the campaign. You may need several hundred volunteers in total to run a successful campaign.

Most organizations engage a consultant to help them run a capital campaign, because this may be the largest amount of money they have ever raised, and they will need expertise that the organization may not have internally. Choosing the right consultant for your organization is critical to your success.

The most likely donors to your campaign will be those who already support your organization. Leadership donor prospects should be brought into the planning phase of the campaign early on so they will feel invested in the project.

Chapter Four

Developing Your Case for Support— Telling Your Story

IN THIS CHAPTER

···➔ What is the case for support and how is it used?

···➔ I've never written a case for support. How do I get started?

···➔ What kind of campaign materials do I need to develop from the case?

···➔ How do I know if our case is compelling to our donors?

One of the first steps in your campaign is to develop a case for this campaign. All organizations should have a case for support for their organization, but if you have not yet developed that case, the campaign is the perfect opportunity for you to develop the organizational case for support from which the campaign case statement will be developed. If there is an organizational case for support in place, this will form the basis of the campaign case statement. This is the first essential ingredient in effectively communicating your needs to your constituents.

A preliminary case statement should be developed before beginning the planning study. Consultants need a written piece of information that outlines the organization's programs and the needs that will be addressed in this campaign that will be shared with the people being interviewed. In general, the preliminary case does not have all the detail and the emotional stories to draw in the readers that the final case will have, but it is important to lay out the plan, the budget, and the opportunities to participate. The preliminary case is often presented as just a few pages of information typed onto an 8½ x 11 sheet of paper. Sometimes it will be presented to interviewees through a booklet format, or through PowerPoint or view book format. But in any case, it should have an "insider" feel. You don't want your preliminary case to look like a final brochure, because you are seeking input on the case from those you interview or survey. The preliminary case statement will then be refined during the study, before it is translated into a final case statement for the campaign.

Case: The reasons why an organization both needs and merits philanthropic support, usually by outlining the organization's programs, currents needs, and plans.

Source: *AFP Fundraising Dictionary*

Those who read your case will want to know the mission and vision of your organization, what the organization does, where it is headed, what its values are, and why it is important to the community.

The history of your organization is important, especially to the degree that the organization can show a track record of success. Most donors don't want to support a project unless they know the organization can deliver what it promises. When an organization can demonstrate it has successfully provided programs and has evaluated its success, donors are motivated to be a part of its future success.

The organizational case for support should outline all your organization's programs and services in detail. The campaign case statement will focus on the programs and services that will be involved in the project. For example, if a college is raising money for a new performing arts center, it would want to focus on the need for expanded programs in that area, the potential audiences for these programs, and the benefit of this new center to the students and community.

Additional items to include in the case are a list of your board and staff. Knowing that the governance of your organization is in the hands of well-known and respected community leaders assures the reader that your organization is governed by people who have the abilities to monitor organization progress and assure that its programs serve the mission. Likewise, a staff possessing the credentials to run the programs is important. A sound financial picture must also be presented. Donors don't want to support a "sinking ship." In the campaign case statement, well thought out projections of the project are important. You may not have an exact budget, but preliminary projections and plans should be laid out for the interviewees to review and comment on. It will also be important to show details of the project, such as the size of the building, the location, and how you will fund the expanded operations in the building, if appropriate.

Some of the key ingredients that will be in the case for support include:

◆ Mission

◆ Vision

◆ History

◆ Current Programs & Services

◆ List of Board and Staff

◆ Financial Information

◆ Need for Growth

◆ Plan for Addressing These Needs

◆ Opportunities for the Donor to Participate in the Vision

 practical tip

Occasionally, an organization uses the planning study to determine the community's opinion on several plans, but you should have a clear idea of its needs and how you plan to address those needs. Your organization cannot go to the public and say, "We think we need more space," without showing that it has evaluated several options and chosen one or two that make the most sense.

There must be a clear need for this project not related to the organization alone, but to the community of which the donor is a part. And there must be a logical plan for addressing the needs.

important

Remember that, to be compelling, a case statement should have a sense of urgency but should never appear "desperate." Remember, too, that the case needs both emotional and rational reasons for the donor to give. Donors are drawn in first by emotion but, before writing a check or signing a pledge card, they want assurance that this plan has been carefully thought out and that it will work.

Perhaps the most important thing to remember when developing the case for support is that it should always be written from the donor's point of view, not your organization's need. What's in it for the donor? How can the donor become involved? There should be various options for donor investment in the project—named giving opportunities, pledges over a period of years, planned giving opportunities, matching gifts. And spell out donor benefits.

important

Who Should Write the Case Statement, and Where Do You Start?

One thing that you should always remember is that there must be one author of the case statement. Although it is wise to get input from a variety of sources, the case will not flow well if several authors with different styles write it. In many instances, consultants will write the case, and sometimes development professionals write it.

The sequence for writing a campaign case statement is:

◆ Develop or review the organizational case for support.

◆ Prepare a preliminary campaign case statement based on the organizational case for support.

◆ Test the preliminary
case statement
through a planning
study or other means.

◆ Prepare the final
campaign case
statement based on
input received during
the planning study.

Occasionally, the case is written by
a public relations firm or marketing
department. However, a word of
caution in these instances is that
the case is a *fundraising* piece, *not*
a publicity piece, and needs to be
written by someone who understands
the psychology and techniques of
fundraising.

◆ Translate the case
statement into
appropriate campaign
materials.

Involving Donors in the Case Statement

The planning study (which will be discussed in more detail in the next
chapter) is the ideal way to test the case statement and to involve donors
in the early phases of its development. A preliminary case statement is
developed to be used when
the consultant interviews
people about their interest
in supporting the campaign.
Sometimes this piece is
referred to as a statement
of need or by other
terminology, but basically it
is the preliminary case. The
preliminary case statement
may not have all the
emotionalism and graphics
that will be in the final
case statement, but it will
have most of the essential

It is essential to have the final case
statement complete before attempting
to develop campaign brochures and
other materials. All campaign materials
must be based on the case statement
in order to present a uniform message
to all constituents. Even though the
materials may be different in format, the
message must be the same.

ingredients listed in the previous issue about case statements, including
opportunities for donors to become involved. An essential element of the
preliminary case is the scale of gifts, showing donors what size gifts are

The table of gifts also shows that all size gifts are important, and that no campaign ever succeeds on the premise of getting "1,000 people to give $1,000." There are always those few who can give at leadership levels; more who can give mid-range gifts; and many who can support the campaign with modest gifts. This is a fact of life in every campaign, and it is important to explain this principle to donors early in the campaign process.

important

needed in order for this campaign to succeed. It is important to involve donors in this process, and to show them that leadership gifts are needed if the campaign is to reach its goal. The study is a good opportunity to stress the need for these leadership gifts and determine if the donor is engaged enough to consider a such a gift.

On rare occasions where a study is not completed prior to a campaign, it will still be important to involve donors in developing the case statement. Some ways this can be done are through personal interviews with selected donors to get their input, or through a series of focus groups where the case can be presented and discussed. Involving donors in developing the case assures that you are on the right track and will help you get buy-in from key donors before launching the campaign. In some instances, you may be heading down a wrong path, unaware that your constituents will not be supportive of the campaign. It is best to learn this before the campaign plan is finalized, than to find out midstream that the community will not support this project. Leadership level donors want to be "in on the ground floor," providing input into your case and on the project itself.

The Final Step in Case Development

The final step to complete the case is taking the information gained in the study, or other processes used to obtain donor input, and finalize the campaign case statement. Sometimes your goals will change, named giving opportunities may be revised, and certain aspects of the program may be given more or less emphasis based on the input received. In most instances, there are not dramatic changes to the case. For example, I once did a study for a fraternity that wanted to raise money to renovate its chapter house, provide building endowment for future needs and put money into a scholarship endowment in order to attract serious students into the fraternity. We wrote the preliminary case based on these three aspects of the campaign. However, after completing the interviews, I found that none of the donors wanted to fund scholarship endowment, because they didn't think that was the role of their local fraternity chapter. The final case was revised to reflect their input, and the campaign was successful.

At this juncture, it is also important to review the case to make sure it contains personal stories that draw the reader in emotionally, as well as a rational explanation of why this campaign is needed and that the plan is solid. You should also gather some dramatic photographs, plans for the building, and other graphics that help illustrate the project.

Once the final internal case is complete, it is now time to think about what kind of campaign materials will effectively present the case. Although you will not be ready to start printing these materials yet, you should think about what types and quantities of materials you will use, so you can develop a realistic campaign budget. Typical campaign materials developed from the case statement include:

◆ Grant applications

◆ Individual donor proposals

◆ Brochures

◆ Pledge cards and letters of intent

◆ Letterhead and envelopes

◆ Response envelopes

◆ Website or web page

◆ Press releases

◆ Campaign newsletters

◆ Speeches

◆ Fact sheets

◆ Question and answer sheets

◆ Volunteer training materials

◆ Solicitation letters

◆ Phone scripts

◆ Named-gift opportunities forms

Remember that different constituents want to see different aspects of the campaign and, although the way the message is presented will

---

I have provided a number of sample documents at the end of the book, in the Appendices, that you will find helpful:

◆ A *Sample Preliminary Case Statement* is provided in **Appendix F.**

◆ A *Sample of a Compelling Emotional Statement from a Case for Support* is provided in **Appendix G.**

◆ A *Sample Emotional/Rational Appeal as Part of the Case* is provided in **Appendix H.**

◆ A *Checklist for Case Statement Evaluation Worksheet* is provided in **Appendix I.**

◆ A *Named Gift Table Worksheet* is provided in **Appendix J.**

◆ A *Campaign Materials Worksheet* is provided in **Appendix K.**

◆ A *Sample Table of Gifts Chart* is provided as **Appendix L.**

For the full-sized PDF files for theses resources, contact the author at:

 http://charitychannel.com/cc/linda-lysakowski

practical tip

vary according to donor needs and expectations, the message must be consistent in all campaign materials.

To Recap

Develop a compelling case for support for the campaign. This process begins by developing a preliminary case for support, which will be tested with your constituents through the planning study or some other method. The case must be both rational and emotional and must be written from the donor's point of view.

It is important that the person responsible for writing the case for support has a good understanding of both the organization and of capital campaign theory and technique.

This case, once finalized, will be developed into different types of campaign materials to appeal to various constituents. It is critical that the materials are not developed independently, but that all come from the source document—the campaign case statement.

Chapter Five

The Planning Study

IN THIS CHAPTER

···→ Do we need to do a planning or feasibility study before we run a campaign?

···→ How long will a study take and how much will it cost?

···→ Can we do a study without a consultant?

···→ What can I do to prepare for a study?

···→ What happens if we don't do a study?

Y ou may have heard the study referred to in different terms, most often the feasibility study, but the more preferred term recently is *planning study*. For many organizations, the study is not done to determine whether they *can* do a capital campaign, but to help them *plan* a successful campaign. Another reason I prefer the use of the term *planning study* is because many people, when hearing the term *feasibility study* think of the architectural feasibility study. Basically a planning study, the term I will use here, is an independent study conducted by a person or firm outside the nonprofit organization, to determine whether the organization is ready for a capital campaign and to provide a timetable and plan that will lead to success.

One thing that distinguishes a capital campaign from other fundraising your organization does is that it is a very public campaign, with an announcement of how much money the organization plans to raise in order to achieve the goals. Often, it is the largest amount of money your organization has ever attempted to raise, and the purpose of the campaign is to implement a building project or build an endowment to fund the organization's future. In other words, you cannot afford to fail!

 practical tip

What Is It? Do You Need One? When?

Some organizations think the only information gained in the study is what dollar goal can be achieved in a campaign. There are many more valuable reasons from conducting a study besides targeting the likely achievement of a financial goal. If you are about to embark on a capital campaign, you should consider a study to avoid the possibility of failure, but also to strengthen your organization internally and help prepare you for the campaign. Even if the study recommends that you are not ready for a campaign, the information gained during the study will help your organization tremendously.

What Will the Study Tell You?

Yes, one of the important outcomes of the study is to tell you if your goal will likely be achieved. But what else can you learn from the study? A well done planning study will assess the organization's internal readiness for a major campaign effort—do you have the infrastructure in place to manage a campaign? Is your board willing to endorse this campaign financially and otherwise? Is your staff capable of running a campaign, and do they have the time to devote to this major effort? Do you have a base of potential donors for the campaign?

The study also tells you about your external public's readiness to support the campaign. Do you have good public relations? Do the key people in your community know who you are and what you do? Is your leadership, both staff and volunteer, known and respected in the community? Are there people who would step up to the plate with a major gift? Are there key community leaders who will jump on board to lead your campaign? The planning study answers all these questions and more.

So, How Does It Work? Who Does the Study?

The planning study should *always* be conducted by an outside consultant who is experienced in conducting studies, and who has the knowledge, the expertise, and the objectivity to provide the organization with valid results and recommendations.

The study begins with the consultant performing an internal assessment of your organization, preparing a preliminary case for support that will be presented to the people who are interviewed, and helping you develop a list of potential interviewees. The consultant usually meets face-to-face with each prospective interviewee and asks them about your organization, your plan, and their willingness to support your campaign. The consultant then prepares an extensive report, listing the qualitative and quantitative results of the interviews, along with recommendations for your organization to either proceed with the campaign as planned, make some adjustments to the plan, or delay the campaign until you are better prepared.

How Long Will It Take? How Much Will It Cost?

In general, the study will take about three to four months and will cost anywhere from $20,000 to $50,000, or even more, depending on factors such as the size of your organization and the campaign, the number and location of the people to be interviewed, and the expenses related the interview process.

What If We Don't Do a Study?

The study does not guarantee that your organization will run a successful campaign. And there are some instances where a study may not be needed, but these are rare. For example, if your organization has a strong commitment from a major donor(s) that 60 to 80 percent of the money is already available, or if the project has a very small dollar goal and the organization has a strong annual fund in place, or your board has committed half to two-thirds of the goal themselves, a study might not be needed. I have consulted for several campaigns that were successful

For most capital campaigns, the study will lay important groundwork to prevent a failed campaign. The study will provide recommendations on strengthening the organization internally, building stronger constituent relationships, and planning a realistic timetable.

practical tip

even though there was no study beforehand. In one instance, the campaign had a goal of $7.2 million, and the three co-chairs had each pledged $1,000,000 or more. These co-chairs had a lot of good connections, so they felt fairly certain they could leverage their own commitments into a successful campaign, and they were absolutely correct. The campaign raised more than $12,000,000. In another case, I consulted for a small campaign (less than $500,000), and this particular group had an urgent need to complete the campaign—their roof had collapsed in a snowstorm, and they needed to raise money quickly to continue running the programs. This campaign was for a community center in a small, very close-knit community, and the campaign was successful because of the volunteer commitment involved.

The Study Process: The Internal Assessment

The planning study is an important step in the campaign process. Almost every organization needs to consider a study before launching their campaign. The study provides you with the means to assess both your internal readiness to do a campaign and the community's willingness to support your campaign.

In earlier chapters, we talked about all the essential ingredients the organization needs to consider in its internal readiness. This chapter will explain how that internal readiness is assessed during a study and how the external readiness for a campaign is assessed.

An internal assessment should address several areas—organizational structure, software, staffing, board issues, policies, and procedures. Sometimes this internal assessment involves a full-blown development audit, other times it is completed as the first step in the planning study. Sometimes, development staff is reluctant to suggest an audit for fear they will not "pass." Engaging a consultant for an audit of the development office should not be viewed as a "witch hunt;" the consultant is not there to find a reason to get rid of staff, but is there to conduct an honest assessment and offer recommendations that will make the organization stronger and prepare it for the campaign. A development audit is not something the organization can do on its own. For the same reason, the organization does not attempt to do its financial audit on its own, the development audit needs an expert outsider to study the development program and prepare an objective report. There are, however, some guidelines that the organization can use to perform a preliminary evaluation of its program.

The consultant will often start with a questionnaire for staff and board members and a review of the entire development program. This is usually followed by interviews with development staff, CEO, board members, and sometimes other staff and volunteers. Areas usually addressed in the audit or internal assessment include:

◆ Development communications—newsletters, solicitation letters, website, etc.

◆ Research methods and results

◆ Basic information on the organization's structure—is it a 501 (c)(3), is it registered with proper state and local authorities, etc.

◆ The role of the board—board organizational charts, position descriptions, committee descriptions, etc.

◆ Staffing in the development office and assignment of duties

◆ Where the development office fits into the overall organizational chart

◆ Results of various fundraising programs, such as special events, direct mail, telephone programs, face to face solicitation

◆ The success of a planned giving program, if one is in place

◆ The success of any previous capital campaigns

◆ Software system, information recording, and reporting

♦ Stewardship acknowledgment and recognition of gifts

♦ The strength of the organization's financial position

♦ Public awareness of the organization

♦ The role of the CEO in fundraising

Some of the key areas that the consultant will analyze regarding your readiness to launch a campaign are:

♦ Does your staff have time to manage a campaign, or are they involved in other tasks, whether development or non-development related. Warning signs such as your staff spending all its time on special events, or development staff that are spending part of their time on development and part on program or other areas of the organization are of concern when preparing for a campaign.

♦ The importance given to the development function within the organization—a development officer that does not report to the CEO or an organization that does not spend money on providing the development office with the necessary tools to perform its job, or one that is reluctant to budget for continuing education for development staff is another sign of trouble.

♦ The size and structure of the board are important keys to success. A small or ineffectual board may be a sign that your community will be reluctant to support a campaign or that the board will not have the necessary contacts to even get interviews with key community leaders.

♦ It is essential to have good systems in place. The campaign might be the first time your organization has had to record multi-year pledges. A system that allows for proper pledge recording and coding will be needed. If your organization does not have a good software system in place, you should implement one prior to launching the campaign.

The internal assessment will take anywhere from several weeks to several months, depending on the complexity of the organization and the depth to which the consultant assesses each aspect of the development program. If your organization has never engaged in a campaign before, a complete development audit may be in order. If your organization feels it has a fairly strong development program, or if there is not sufficient time to engage in a full-blown audit, sometimes an abbreviated version is called for during the study process, and a full development audit may take place after the study is complete.

Whichever method used to complete this task, it is essential that some type of internal assessment of the organization's ability to run a campaign be completed before moving on to the external assessment.

important

The Study Process: The External Assessment

Once your organization has determined it is internally ready to run a capital campaign, the next step is performing an external assessment of whether the community is willing and able to support your project.

The study should always be performed by outside counsel. Interviewees will generally be reluctant to speak frankly to a representative of the organization about its case. Also, a professional who is experienced in studies will need to analyze the data and provide objective recommendations.

The planning study is the most common way organizations assess their community's ability and willingness to support their campaign. The planning study helps your organization determine if the key factors for success are present—sufficient leadership gifts, key community leaders willing to serve in leadership roles in the campaign, and a compelling case for support.

important

If you have a limited budget you should consider outside counsel for the study, even if you feel you could run the campaign yourself.

Once a consultant is engaged for the study, that consultant will work with you to determine which key players to interview during the study. In most cases, anywhere from thirty-five to fifty persons will be interviewed. Sometimes it will be necessary to interview more people, due to the size or scope of your campaign. Occasionally a study will involve fewer interviews if the goal is very small.

Some categories of people who should be interviewed include:

> Interviewing the *right* people is more important than the number of interviews. Generally the organization develops a list of seventy-five to one hundred people, and then the consultant and the steering committee review that list and sort the names by categories, A, B, and C, the A list being those who *absolutely must* be interviewed, the B list those who *should* be interviewed, and the C list those who *could* be interviewed.

important

◆ Top donors to the organization

◆ Potential major donors for the organization

◆ Key board members

◆ Key staff people

◆ Community leaders

◆ Key volunteers

◆ Political leaders, especially if you anticipate government support of the project

Once the list of interviewees is developed, letters are sent first to the A List, and then interviews are scheduled with those people. These are followed by the B list and then the C list, if necessary, to complete the number of interviews needed. Be aware, however that this list is fluid. Often during the interview process, new names will surface that were not on any of the previous lists, but that interviewees identify as people who would have the interest and ability to make a major gift to the campaign.

Interviews may be scheduled by the organization or by the consultant, depending on the terms of the contract. It is generally best to have a person who has some familiarity and influence with the interviewee schedule the interview. This is often the most challenging part of the process—getting the interview. While most major donors and community leaders are familiar with the process and usually agree to interviews, it is sometimes difficult to get onto their busy schedules. The person scheduling the interview needs to be creative and persistent in making calls, sometimes calling early in the morning before the "gatekeeper" answering the phone comes to work, or if the organization has access to the person's cell number and email, this can also be effective.

Once the interview is scheduled, a confirmation letter is generally sent along with the preliminary case statement so the interviewee has an opportunity to become familiar with the case before the consultant arrives for the interview. In most cases, the consultants will interview people in their home or office, as there are often clues about the person's ability and interests in those surroundings. For example, I recall interviewing a retired United States Senator and former Cabinet member, whom the organization assumed would be a lead donor to the campaign. As soon as I walked into the Senator's home I spotted a gallery of photos covering an entire wall of his living room. During the conversation as I asked about his commitment to the campaign, he pointed to his "gallery" and said, "Educating those fourteen grandchildren is my number one priority." I knew he would make a significant gift to the campaign, but not at the level the organization had hoped—not because he felt no close bond to this organization, but obviously he had an even closer bond to his grandchildren.

Also, most people are more likely to speak freely when they feel they are in control of the surroundings. During the interviews, the consultant will ask interviewee opinions on the organization itself, the strength of the case, the interviewee's propensity to make a

I have provided a number of sample documents at the end of the book, in the Appendices, that you will find helpful:

♦ A *Sample Questions Asked During Planning Study Interviews* is provided in **Appendix M.**

♦ A *Sample Table of Contents of a Study Report* is provided in **Appendix N.**

♦ A *Sample Qualitative and Quantitative Comments from a Study Report* is provided in **Appendix O.**

practical tip

major gift, willingness to serve in a leadership role in the campaign, and for suggestions for other donors and/or volunteers to the campaign. Most people are more at ease being asked these probing questions in their own comfort zone.

The consultants will then prepare a report for your leadership outlining the qualitative and quantitative responses to the questions asked, and their recommendation whether to move forward with a campaign, along with a proposed time schedule for the campaign. If the recommendation is that you are not ready, the consultant will provide advice on what you need to do to better prepare for a campaign. The consultant often prepares several versions of the report—a complete report you will share with the steering committee, an executive summary that is distributed to the board and key staff people, and a brief summary report to be mailed or emailed to those who took part in the interview process.

To Recap

Most campaigns start with a planning study to determine both their internal readiness to conduct a campaign and their constituents' readiness to support the campaign. A consultant should be engaged early in the planning process to conduct this study.

The study usually takes about three to four months to complete and will include preparation of the preliminary case statement.

Interviewees must be carefully selected to represent a cross section of community leaders, major donor prospects, and key individuals in your organization.

Sometimes a full-blown development audit is conducted before a consultant is engaged to do the planning study.

Chapter Six

The Campaign Plan and Budget

IN THIS CHAPTER

···→ What does it mean when people say the campaign must be won on paper first?

···→ How much will it cost to run our campaign?

···→ How long will it take to run the campaign?

Once your organization has completed a planning study and decides to proceed with the campaign, the first step in that process is to develop a campaign plan outlining the entire structure of the campaign. If you are working with a consultant, generally the consultant will develop the plan. If there is no consultant involved, you should make certain that there is someone on staff who has worked on a capital campaign before and has the ability to develop a campaign plan. As I mentioned before, the campaign plan is essential, and you might want to consider engaging a consultant to develop the plan and then see if you can implement it on your own.

The campaign plan is the foundation for a successful campaign and will help you get things off to a good start. The plan should include a brief overview of the process that led to the decision to conduct a campaign. A key ingredient of the plan is the campaign organizational chart showing all the various divisions of the campaign and the number of committee people needed to staff all the divisions. Position descriptions for all volunteers should also be included in the plan, along with a timeline for each committee and an overall time schedule. The campaign budget is also part of the plan. Volunteers should not be recruited until the plan is completed. It is critical to show volunteers that a well-thought-out plan, including expectations of volunteers has been developed, so they understand their role and the time and monetary expectations. The principle groups of volunteers that will be involved are members of the campaign cabinet, which includes chairs of all the various committees that will be involved in the campaign.

Campaign Divisions

Determining the divisions that will be included in your campaign is the first step in the plan. In every campaign there will be a leadership gifts division, a major gifts division, along with one or more general community appeal division. Sometimes, depending on the size of the campaign and the scale of gifts needed to achieve the goal, there may be other categories based on the size of gifts, such as special gifts. Once the leadership and major donor prospects are identified, you will probably want to break out the divisions by categories of constituents, and then within these divisions will be different levels of giving. For example, a school might have a parents division, an alumni division, and a "friends of the school" division. Or a membership organization might have a division that will contact its members. Or, if your organization is national in scope, you may have regional divisions based on geographic location. There is often a civic and professional organization division that will contact local community groups for their support as an organization. Also, a foundation division is generally in place to coordinate the approach to foundations, and a small business division to contact businesses in the community.

Other Campaign Committees

In addition to the various campaign divisions that will be directly involved in soliciting donors, several other committees will be included on the campaign organizational chart. There is generally a prospect evaluation committee, whose task will be to identify and evaluate prospects and assign them to the proper divisions. Most campaigns also have a public relations committee to handle media relations for the campaign and the development of campaign materials, but sometimes this is handled through internal staff or the PR committee of the board. There will also be several campaign-related events, such as a kickoff celebration, a groundbreaking and dedication, and open house event, and all of these events will need volunteers. Usually there is a main events committee on the campaign chart, and that chair will recruit different people to work on each event. Cultivation events are usually held as a part of the campaign process, as well, and these usually fall under the events committee.

If you do not have a finance department or a finance committee of the board to handle things like the campaign budget and financing options, you might need to establish a special committee to handle this part of your campaign. It will be critical to have staff or volunteers involved who can develop the project budget, negotiate short term financing for the construction phase of the project, and develop investment policies for gifts received. Likewise, if you don't already have a facilities committee in your organization, a committee to handle the actual construction may be part of the campaign cabinet. Again, if you do not have people on your staff with experience in construction, you should engage some high level volunteers with experience in this area.

Some organizations may have other committees as well; for example churches and faith based organizations usually have a prayer committee as part of their campaign cabinet. You might also want a committee to deal with stewardship and donor recognition. Some groups also have a special committee to work with soliciting gifts in kind for the project. If your project will involve a number of governmental funding sources, you may want a committee to deal with this facet of the campaign, as well.

> Each committee that will be involved in directly soliciting prospective donors should have its own goals within the campaign goal and this should be spelled out in the campaign plan as well as an overall scale of gifts showing how many gifts at each level will be needed.

practical tip

Other Items in the Campaign Plan

Other important parts of the campaign plan are gift acceptance policies and recognition policies. It is vital to have these before launching the campaign.

It will be necessary to have these things in place before asking volunteers to make calls. Otherwise, you could face issues like a volunteer who is excited about getting a major gift of land only to learn that your organization cannot accept this and, because it needs soil remediation, is not in a part of town that is convenient for your clients, or does not have access to public transportation, etc.

> One of the worst experiences for a volunteer can be when they successfully solicit a gift and then learn that the gift is not acceptable to the organization, or that the way the donor wishes to be recognized is not in conformity with organizational policies.
>
> **observation**

Having the plan in place and assuring that it is followed will make any campaign flow smoother. Like the planning study, it is one of the essential building blocks of a successful campaign. And, again, if an organization is on a tight budget, it may be wise to pay a consultant to develop the plan and then implement the plan on its own, or with limited guidance from the consultant.

The Campaign Budget

There are two budget areas that must be considered when embarking on a capital campaign—the project budget and the campaign budget.

Project Costs

If, of course, the project does not involve construction, the budget will be very different for the project itself, but if the project does involve construction, the architect or construction manager will generally help develop the budget for the building project. This budget will include items such as:

◆ Construction costs (sometimes called hard costs, soft costs being items like fees and permits)

◆ Architectural fees (usually a percentage of the project)

◆ Architectural renderings (these need to be done before the project is started and the costs should be funded up front, because these drawings are important in presenting the case)

◆ Engineering and contractor fees

◆ Fees and permits required by local municipalities

◆ Environmental impact studies (and historical impact studies if the building involves a historical structure)

◆ Possible environmental cleanup if issues are found such as asbestos removal or soil remediation

◆ FF&E (furniture, fixtures and equipment)

◆ Communication systems (telephone, Internet)

◆ Computer systems, including wiring

◆ Possibly rental for office space during construction phase

◆ Loan interest for construction or bridge loan while pledges are being paid

◆ Inflation—the longer the project is delayed, the higher expenses will be.

◆ Contingency for unexpected expenses

Campaign Costs

Campaign expenses are in a separate category and are usually funded through the campaign itself. If your organization's operating budget allows for covering campaign expenses, the entire campaign dollars raised can go directly into the project. However, in most organizations, these expenses are folded into the overall goal for the campaign. Fundraising costs are dependent on many factors, such as the size of the campaign, the duration of the campaign, the geographic scope of the campaign, the amount of time required from a consultant, and the existing fundraising structure in place within your organization. However, as a general rule of thumb, these costs will run somewhere between 5 and 15 percent of the total campaign goal, and usually the larger the campaign, the lower this percentage will be.

These campaign costs include:

◆ Personnel—If your organization needs to hire extra staff to manage the campaign, you will need to budget for salaries, benefits, and employment taxes for this person or persons.

◆ Professional counsel—Might include a campaign consultant, a grant writer, a public relations consultant, and outside bookkeeping services. Travel expense must also be considered if engaging counsel from outside your locality. The organization should be sure that proposals from consultants include all anticipated expenses. Does the consultant require housing while on site? Will there be rental cars, airfare, and mileage expenses? You should check with your state regulatory authorities to make sure the consultant contracts comply with state laws and that the counsel being engaged is registered in your state, if registration is required.

◆ Marketing expense will include graphic design, photography, printing of brochures, letterhead and envelopes, website, campaign video. If you are planning to use a telephone fundraising firm, this cost should also be included.

A word of caution on engaging telephone consulting firms, you should look for firms that work on a flat fee basis, not percentage-based fees, which is unethical according to AFP standards. In many states, firms are required to disclose their fee if they work on a percentage basis.

watch out!

◆ Donor recognition items and events also should be budgeted for and planned early in the campaign so donors can be advised of what type of recognition they will receive.

◆ Campaign events, including cultivation events, kickoff event, report meetings, groundbreaking and dedication events must be budgeted as well. Event expenses will generally include facility rental (unless you are using your own facility), food, entertainment, equipment rental, supplies, and possibly an event director (this fee may be included with professional counsel).

◆ Support Systems—If you need to purchase software, you can do this through the campaign or through your general operating budget, since the system will be used for ongoing development operations. Other systems expenses will include telephone, fax, and Internet

---

I have provided a number of sample documents at the end of the book, in the Appendices, that you will find helpful:

◆ A *Sample Volunteer Plan* is provided in **Appendix P.**

◆ A *Sample Breakdown of Scale of Gifts by Division* is provided in **Appendix Q.**

◆ A *Sample Breakdown of Campaign Elements* is provided in **Appendix R.**

◆ A *Sample Full Campaign Timeline* is provided in **Appendix S.**

◆ A *Sample Campaign Organization Chart* in **Appendix T.**

◆ A *Sample Campaign Budget* is provided in **Appendix U.**

For the full-sized PDF files for theses resources, contact the author at:

 http://charitychannel.com/cc/
linda-lysakowski

 practical tip

directly related to the campaign. Postage and office supplies are also charged to the campaign.

◆ Travel expenses may also be a factor if the campaign is regional or national in scope, or if trips to national or regional foundations are required.

The campaign budget should be developed during the campaign planning phase and monitored on a monthly basis.

To Recap

It is critical to develop the campaign plan in writing before you start to invite volunteers to get involved and before contacting prospective donors.

This plan should include an organizational chart, job descriptions for staff, volunteers, and consultants, as well as a campaign budget and detailed timeline.

You will need both a project budget for the actual construction and a budget for campaign costs. Most organizations include campaign costs when establishing their campaign goal.

Chapter Seven

Recruiting and Organizing Campaign Volunteers

IN THIS CHAPTER

---→ How important are volunteers in the campaign?

---→ How many volunteers will I need to recruit?

---→ Where can I find enough volunteers?

O nce the campaign plan is in place, the organization can start recruiting volunteers to help implement the plan. While the role of staff and board are important during the campaign, the role of volunteers is critical to success and should not be undervalued.

Involving key community leaders in the campaign will assure that the entire community gets involved.

The chair should be someone who has passion to speak with enthusiasm about the project and your organization. Leadership qualities are also

Recruiting the right campaign chair is the first step in getting community leaders involved. A chair who is well known and respected in the community will be able to use that influence to recruit other community leaders to come on board.

practical tip

important, as the campaign chair needs to motivate and inspire all the other volunteers who will be involved.

In many cases, there will be two co-chairs of a campaign or a chair and vice chair. Occasionally it is wise to have more than two people head up a campaign, particularly if there are spouses involved. You should carefully evaluate the reasons to include more than one person as chair, as this will require a little more coordination, and clear roles should be defined for each person in a leadership role. It is critical to recruit the chair before enlisting other volunteers, because people will be reluctant to get involved if they don't know who will direct their efforts. The right campaign chair(s) can be very influential in recruiting other volunteers.

I consulted for one organization that had a very successful campaign, mainly because they had an excellent chairperson. This key community leader was originally approached to be the honorary chair of the campaign, because the organization thought he would not be able to commit much time to the campaign. He agreed to serve as honorary chair but attended every campaign meeting, presided over the meetings, agreed to ask some of his friends and associates to contribute and was very enthused about the whole project. Bringing him on board early on in the campaign made it very easy to recruit other volunteers. He owned the largest manufacturing company in the community and was very well respected in the community. We sent a letter signed by him to other key community leaders, including the presidents of four major banks, all of whom agreed to serve on the campaign cabinet.

On the other hand, one organization I know had a campaign that really floundered, because they had a chairperson who was influential in the community but did not devote time to the campaign. She missed meetings, showed up late, and was reluctant to ask her friends to contribute. The choice of the right chair can make a campaign successful—the wrong chair can cause a campaign to end in disaster.

Many organizations find it helpful to have an honorary chair of the campaign in addition to the chair(s). An honorary chair generally does not have many campaign duties, but his or her presence should be expected at major campaign events. Often using this key community leader's name on your campaign letterhead is enough to show the community that you have some influential people supporting your project. You should expect your honorary chair to review the plan and offer advice, attend the kickoff and dedication events and offer to sign letters. You can also ask the honorary chair to speak to friends and colleagues about the campaign. Some honorary chairs really "get into" the campaign and attend campaign meetings, make solicitation calls, and help identify potential donors.

Once the campaign chair is in place, the other campaign cabinet positions can be filled. Working with the organizational structure described in the previous chapter, chairs must be recruited for each division. It is strongly recommended that each division have two co-chairs. Sharing the workload makes it easier to get people to agree to chair a division, and helps assure attendance at campaign cabinet meetings by at least one of the chairs.

Division chairs must be carefully selected to suit the needs of the committees they will be heading. For example, the chairs of the leadership gifts division should be people who will make a leadership level gift themselves and have the contacts and influence to talk with others with leadership gift capability. Likewise, chairs of the special event committee should be well-organized and know how to run a successful event. Each

> Be careful about asking political leaders to serve as the honorary chair of your campaign. Even popular political figures usually have some enemies who could be among your major donor prospects. Another caution is that political and other highly public figures could become involved in real or perceived scandalous behavior that can result in bad publicity for your campaign. In most cases, community donors will respect the fact that you have support from influential people, but choose your honorary chair very carefully.

important

committee chair prospect should be discussed with the campaign chair(s) to determine if this person has the right qualities and if the chair(s) feel this candidate is a good choice for that specific division.

It is critical to have developed the position descriptions and timelines for each committee before recruiting chairs of those committees. Review the plan with the chairperson first, and discuss with the campaign chair possible chairpersons for each position. It is important to recruit chairpersons with whom the campaign chair feels comfortable. The chairs of each committee will then recruit enough volunteers to handle the task they have accepted. Committees that conduct face-to-face solicitation should always follow the rule of one volunteer for every five prospects they will see. In some cases, especially at the leadership gifts level, solicitors may even call on fewer than five people, because the size of the gifts solicited will require numerous visits before the person is prepared to make a commitment. Depending on the number of constituents in the division, it may be necessary to have a structure of team leaders within the division who will recruit additional volunteers. For example, if the small business division has five hundred prospects to solicit, they will need one-hundred volunteers, so rather than have the chairs try to recruit one-hundred volunteers for their division, they can recruit twenty team leaders who will in turn each recruit five volunteers, thereby assuring that all prospects can be visited personally.

There are often hundreds of volunteers involved in a campaign. Although this sometimes sounds like a daunting task to staff and volunteer leadership, the task can be accomplished easily if the organizational structure is in place from the beginning. Following a simple step-by-step process makes this task very easy to accomplish:

- ❑ Establish the campaign divisions, based on the constituents of the organization and the scale of gifts.

- ❑ Determine the number of prospects in each division.

- ❑ Determine the number of volunteers needed to accomplish these solicitations (number of prospects divided by five).

- ❑ Recruit the chair and vice chair of each division.

- ❑ Determine if team leaders are needed, and assist chairs to recruit them.

- ❑ Have team leaders recruit volunteers.

The campaign cabinet needs to meet regularly—monthly, bimonthly, or quarterly, depending on the size and scope of the campaign. Subcommittees should meet individually between meetings. It is very important to have regularly scheduled meetings for committees to report on progress, discuss developments within the organization and the project, and inspire and motivate volunteers. Regular communications between meetings are important, as well. Staff and campaign leadership should be in communication by phone and/or email to assess progress and assure that committees are following the strategies for keeping the campaign on track. It is important for volunteers to celebrate campaign successes, both small and large. And at the end of the campaign there should be a volunteer celebration event.

> Once all volunteers are recruited for each division, they will need to be trained in techniques of making the "ask." Even volunteers who have a lot of campaign experience will need to attend strategy sessions and help develop the appropriate strategies to solicit prospects. Committees working on various divisions in most cases should be trained separately, since the approach to solicit a leadership donor will be very different from that for those in the small business division, for example.

important

Sample Campaign Chair Position Description

The campaign chair is the acknowledged and recognized leader of the capital campaign, who personally subscribes to and supports the financial goals of the campaign and encourages and stimulates the capabilities and generosity of others. A campaign cabinet will assist enlistment of committee leadership. All leadership will be accountable to the campaign chair for the performance of their responsibilities.

Be the official spokesperson for the campaign

◆ Chair the campaign cabinet meetings.

◆ Provide leadership to the various committee kick-off meetings.

◆ Provide leadership and assistance, as needed, in soliciting leadership, major, business, foundation, and individual gifts.

◆ Work with campaign counsel and campaign director to bring the campaign to a successful conclusion and on schedule.

The campaign chair is the representative of the organization's campaign and reflects its values, ideals, and objectives. The chair brings status, inspiration, and motivation to the campaign.

Sample Campaign Vice-Chair Position Description

The campaign vice-chair is the chief assistant to the chair of the capital campaign, who personally subscribes to and supports the financial goals of the campaign and encourages and stimulates the capabilities and generosity of others. A campaign cabinet will assist enlistment of committee leadership. All leadership will be accountable to the campaign chair and vice-chair for the performance of their responsibilities.

◆ In the absence of the chair, serve as the official spokesperson for the campaign.

◆ In the absence of the chair, chair the campaign cabinet meetings.

◆ Assist the chair in providing leadership to the various committee kick-off meetings.

◆ Provide leadership and assistance, as needed, in soliciting leadership, major, business, foundation, and individual gifts.

◆ Work with campaign chair, campaign counsel, and campaign director to bring the campaign to a successful conclusion and on schedule.

The campaign vice-chair is a leading representative of the organization's campaign and reflects its values, ideals, and objectives. The vice-chair brings status, inspiration, and motivation to the campaign.

Sample Honorary Campaign Chair Position Description

The honorary campaign chair is the acknowledged and recognized honorary leader of the capital campaign, who personally subscribes to and supports the financial goals of the campaign and encourages and stimulates the capabilities and generosity of others.

◆ Be the honorary spokesperson for the campaign.

◆ Set the example through outstanding leadership for the community or through exemplary giving in support of the campaign.

The honorary campaign chair is the representative of the organization's campaign and reflects its values, ideals, and objectives. The honorary chair brings status, inspiration, and motivation to the campaign.

Sample Campaign Cabinet Member Position Description

The campaign cabinet is responsible for guiding all aspects of the campaign. The campaign cabinet should be comprised of community leaders—board members, staff, donors, and others who are recognized community leaders. An outline of key leadership positions as well as a general position description for all campaign cabinet members follows.

Members of the capital campaign cabinet provide leadership and direction for the campaign. Members will be recruited from the organization's constituents and will have the following responsibilities, in addition to the responsibilities outlined in the position description of the position filled on the campaign cabinet:

◆ Serve as chair, co-chair, or member of one of the campaign cabinet subcommittees.

◆ Recruit others to serve on various committees, as needed.

◆ Make a meaningful gift to the campaign.

◆ Identify and solicit possible leadership and major donors to the campaign.

◆ Attend campaign events and functions.

◆ Attend monthly meetings of the campaign cabinet.

◆ Promote the campaign in the community.

To Recap

Volunteer leadership is one of the most critical aspects of a successful campaign. Start by recruiting the right campaign chair or preferably co-chairs. You might also want to consider an honorary chair.

Always follow the five-to-one rule when determining how many volunteers you need in each division. Volunteers who make personal visits to prospective donors should not be asked to call on more than five prospects.

All campaign volunteers need orientation and should be trained immediately before they are scheduled to make their calls. Ongoing report meetings are important to keep the process moving in a timely manner and to keep volunteers motivated.

Chapter Eight

Identifying and Cultivating Donors

IN THIS CHAPTER

···→ Where do we find new donors for our campaign?

···→ How much money can we reasonably expect to get from our existing donor base?

···→ What if the major funders in our area are not familiar with our organization?

A s mentioned in the beginning of this book, one of the key ingredients of a successful campaign is having a pool of donors to solicit.

For many organizations, this is fairly easy—perhaps they have a solid base of steady donors, an alumni, or list of grateful service recipients. For others, this task may be more challenging because they have no donor history or built in pool of donors. However, every organization has people with a vested interest in that organization's success. The trick is determining who they are, what their ability is, and what their level of commitment is to your organization.

One mistake many organizations make is thinking they need to go out and find a whole new group of donors for their capital campaign, because they don't want to ask their loyal donors once again. Or, sometimes organizations think they can raise all the money they need for their capital project through grants. While grants will usually play an important part in the campaign process, it is important to remember that over 80 percent of all contributions to charitable organizations come from individuals. Another important principle of fundraising is that the most likely donors to the capital campaign will be those who already support your organization.

watch out!

The first place to start is with the "family" of your organization—board, staff, and others close to your organization. It will be crucial to have 100 percent board commitment before asking others to support the project. Each board member should be solicited personally, on a face-to-face basis. You will need the board appeal committee as part of your campaign cabinet. This committee should carefully evaluate the board potential, keeping in mind that they will be asking each board member to make a stretch gift. The board chair should lead the way in making the first gift to the campaign and should stress at board meetings the importance of board giving. As with any fundraising appeal, the board gifts should be completed before asking anyone else to contribute. If you work with a consultant, that person can help emphasize to the board that others in the community will not contribute until the board has one hundred percent commitment.

A staff appeal should also be held early in the campaign to show the public that the family of your organization has given its full support. Some organizations hesitate to invite staff members to contribute, feeling that nonprofit employees are "overworked and underpaid." However, staff must be made to feel they are part of the campaign. One way to approach the staff is to offer them payroll deduction for their pledge payments, making it easier to contribute. Staff members may also have spouses who work for companies that will match their gifts, so all of these options should be considered. Appoint a committee of staff members to handle the staff appeal, the chairs of which will serve on the campaign cabinet. In larger organizations, each department has a subcommittee of people working on the campaign. In some organizations, departments compete with each other to raise the most money or get the highest percentage of pledges, offering incentives in the form of a department pizza party, a day off, etc. Staff members can hold events to raise money, but this can take a lot of time from the staff's regular work schedule. The best approach is to ask each employee to make an individual pledge that counts towards their department's overall goal.

If your organization has an annual giving history, the first place to start is by searching your donor records. Using a good donor software system will facilitate this task. First run a list of the top 10 percent of your organization's donors. These are good prospects for lead gifts. Another key is searching the records for loyal donors, those who have given consistently to

One thing to be careful about when conducting a staff appeal is to assure that no one feels pressured into making a gift. To prevent any feeling of pressure or harassment, bosses should never solicit their employees for a gift. You can have committee members from one department solicit employees in another department to avoid any potential conflict.

watch out!

your organization, even if not at significant levels. Often these donors have never been asked to give at a higher level, or have not been aware of the bigger vision of your organization.

Your Organization's Alumni

Even those organizations that think they don't have alumni or a built in constituent base will probably have a pool of prospects that are close to the organization.

Volunteers are another good source for campaign donations. Many organizations hesitate to ask their volunteers for money, knowing they are giving of their time. However, remember that a person's time is often more precious to them than their money, and if they are giving of their

Many organizations have "alumni," groups of people who have received services or have given service to the organization. Those who have given blood, adopted animals, hold a library card, etc. are likely donors when the organization launches a capital campaign.

important

time, they are likely to want to support your organization financially, as well. Your organization's vendors are another likely donor pool.

If you cannot identify a pool of natural prospects, the campaign cabinet and board should be called upon to help identify prospects who, after some cultivation, might be prospective donors.

Cultivating Prospective Donors

Once a pool of prospective donors is identified, your campaign leadership needs to determine each prospect's readiness to be asked for a gift. If it is determined that the prospect is not familiar with or enthused enough about the organization's mission, the campaign committee should plan an appropriate cultivation strategy for each prospect. Cultivation can include one-on-one meetings, invitations to tour the organization's facilities, or a meeting with agency leadership. Group cultivation events may also be used, such as having a board or cabinet member host a small cocktail party in their home, bringing the prospects in for a breakfast or luncheon in the organization facility, or other such events. The events committee of your campaign cabinet can be called upon to help plan group events. The members of the leadership gifts and major gifts committees may also want to plan one-on-one cultivation for the committee's prospective donors. During the cultivation period, donors are not asked to donate, but are provided with information, presented with the case for support, and provided an opportunity to meet those who benefit from the organization's services.

Cultivation may take several months or several years in some cases, depending on the amount of the gift and the level of interest the prospect has in the organization. In some cases, the prospect may not be ready to make a gift for this campaign, but cultivation for the future is important, even if there is not a significant gift at this time. Patient cultivation for major gifts is better than rushing the prospect into a

A Sample Brainstorming Form to Identify New Donors is provided in **Appendix V.**

practical tip

decision that may result in a smaller gift and a lack of commitment to the organization's vision for the future.

To Recap

The most likely donors for your campaign will be those who are already supporting financially the organization and/or through volunteer efforts. Every organization has a pool of people who could be considered "alumni," those who have benefited from the services your organization provides. Start with the family of your organization— board and staff—and then move on to your best donors, your volunteers and vendors.

If these prospective donors do not know enough about your organization or the campaign, some patient cultivation will pay huge dividends. Rather than just going out and asking before a prospect is ready to give, plan some one-on-one cultivation and/or cultivation events for groups of prospective donors.

Chapter Nine

Making the Ask

T he structure is in place, the case has been written, the volunteers have been recruited, and the donor prospects are identified. All that remains now is to make the "ask."

Who makes the "ask," when, how, and for how much?

First, let's talk about the right person. Finding the right person to make the "ask" is critical. This is why the prospects are identified and rated in screening sessions with the campaign cabinet and other volunteers. The key to a major gift lies in three key ingredients:

◆ Linkage

◆ Ability

◆ Interest

> It is said that the key to a successful gift is having the right person ask the right person, at the right time, in the right way, for the right amount, and for the right reason. Perhaps easier said than done.
>
> **observation**

During the screening and rating sessions, it will be essential to find the best "asker." While several people on the committee might know the prospective donor, the committee must identify the person with the best connection to the prospect.

The ability of the prospect must also be considered in order to make sure the "ask amount" is right. Research into past donor giving history, the prospect's history of giving to other organizations, and an estimate of the prospect's assets will help determine the ask amount. Staff can research this formally, but a lot of information is gathered during the screening and rating sessions.

The prospect's interest should also be considered, particularly when the individual is a major donor prospect. Is there a named gift opportunity that fits this prospect's interest? It will be important to discuss the various named giving opportunities during the solicitation call. Often the opportunity to name a building, an area of a building, or a room after a loved one will be the right motivation to get a donor to raise their sights.

Timing is also important and, during the screening process, it should be determined whether the prospect is ready to be solicited or if more cultivation is needed before making the "ask." Remember that gifts should always be solicited with the donor's interests in mind.

Volunteer Training

The volunteers who will be directly involved in soliciting donors should be trained in how best to make the "ask." Staff, volunteers or a consultant can do training. In most cases, it is wise to bring in a consultant to train volunteers. One reason to do this is that the consultant will be able to tell volunteers how important it is for them to make their own gift first. The consultant should be skilled at helping volunteers develop an approach that uses their own unique style to present the case. Role-playing is often used during this training, and the trainer must be skilled in facilitating the role-play.

Some of the key points to cover with volunteers during the training sessions are:

◆ Solicitors must make their own gift first;

◆ Knowing the case and being able to talk passionately about it is critical;

◆ Team solicitations are generally the best approach for major gifts;

◆ The team needs to rehearse their approach beforehand, including determining which one will make the "ask;"

◆ Getting the appointment is sometimes the hardest part of the call, so the person who has the best contact with the prospect should schedule the appointment;

◆ When scheduling an appointment with a couple, make sure both are available for the meeting;

◆ After a brief period of small talk, the solicitation team should present the case, using the campaign materials that have been developed, but speaking with enthusiasm about the organization and its needs, and telling the prospect about how this project meets their interest;

◆ The solicitors must be prepared to demonstrate their own financial commitment to the campaign;

◆ When it is determined that the time is right, one of the solicitors will make the 'ask;'

◆ Always ask for a specific amount, the amount that has been determined in advance of the call;

◆ The way the "ask" is phrased is important—use words like investment or joining us in this vision, rather than asking for a donation;

◆ Once the "ask" is made, the solicitors should remain silent and wait for the prospect to react;

◆ The solicitors should be prepared to answer any questions the prospect has, or be willing to get the answers to those questions;

◆ If the donor says no, the solicitors should probe for the reasons. Is it "no, not that amount," "no, not now," or "no, not for that project."

◆ Solicitors should not leave a pledge card or letter of intent with for the prospect to return by mail, since this usually results in a lower gift or no gift at all. Rather, they should make an appointment to make a second visit to the prospect to collect their signed pledge form;

◆ Follow-up is vital to success. A thank you note should be sent, along with any information the prospect requested.

Training for all volunteers is important. Those calling on a business should be given as much information as possible about the business's relationship with the organization, if there is one. Business people will also be less likely to have an extended conversation about the organization, but will be interested in basic facts about the project benefit to the community. In some cases, volunteers will also be involved in making a follow up presentation to foundations to which the organization has submitted a formal proposal. If calls are made to a foundation, the volunteers should be aware of that foundations' areas of interest and guidelines for making grants. Strategy sessions in preparation for a business or foundation call are as important as they are with individuals.

Some campaigns will also include a phonathon to selected prospects, such as alumni. Volunteers for telephone fundraising also need training in how to best make the "ask" over the phone. Training should be provided the day of the phonathon and should include all volunteers who will be on the phones. Key elements of making "the ask" by phone are:

◆ A pre-call letter should always be sent;

◆ Letters should be signed by a volunteer, rather than a staff person;

◆ Prospects for Phonathons should be people who have a relationship with the organization;

◆ A script should be prepared, however volunteers should be trained to speak from the heart in a natural tone, rather than reading the script word for word;

◆ Callers should confirm that the prospect has received the pre-call letter and ask if they have any questions;

◆ As with major donor fundraising, the caller should always ask for a specific amount and not be too ready to accept a lower amount, but should offer the donor various options such as multi-year pledge, matching gifts, group gifts, etc.

◆ Always thank the prospect, whether a gift is made or not;

◆ Be sure to send a follow-up letter to those who have pledged, those who are considering a pledge, and those who said no, not right now, but may consider gift in the future.

> A Sample Guidelines for Naming Opportunities is provided in **Appendix X.**
>
> A Sample Community Center Capital Campaign Named Giving Opportunities chart is provided in **Appendix Y.**
>
> A Sample Named Gift Opportunities for a Life Sciences Center is provided in **Appendix Z.**
>
>  practical tip

Solicitor Tips

◆ After you have made the formal "ask," remain silent until the prospect has fully responded.

◆ When soliciting for a major gift, don't off a pledge period longer than the campaign pledge schedule—that's a negotiating point.

◆ Don't disagree with a donor's negativism. Validate it and move on!

◆ Select you words thoughtfully:

❖ Instead of "contribute," substitute the word "invest."

❖ Don't ask for a gift, extend an invitation. "I would like to invite you...."

❖ Rather than saying, "Your gift makes a difference," consider, "Gifts such as yours have allowed us to...."

❖ Instead of saying, "Would you consider increasing your gift?" explain the importance of increased gifts. "A 20 percent increase will help us keep pace with...."

◆ Avoid these solicitation errors:

❖ Not asking for a specific amount.

❖ Not asking for a large enough amount.

❖ Not talking about donor benefits.

❖ Not listening—talking too much.

❖ Not asking questions.

❖ Not knowing enough about the prospect before solicitation.

❖ Not being flexible—having alternatives.

❖ Not cultivating the donor before soliciting.

❖ Asking for the gift too soon.

❖ Not knowing enough facts about your organization.

◆ Before making a call, ask yourself three times "why" the prospect should make this gift.

◆ Try to anticipate a prospect's objections by answering them in your presentation.

◆ The best solicitation occurs when the right person is asked for the right gift by the right solicitor at the right time.

◆ Cultivation involves a series of well planned "moves" that bring the prospect from *awareness* to *interest* to *involvement* and, finally, to *commitment.*

◆ When soliciting a married couple, pay equal attention to both spouses. The most vocal of the two isn't always the one who makes the final decision.

◆ If prospects are well cultivated, highly motivated, and effectively solicited, then they could be expected to contribute 5 percent of annual income over a five-year period, or 10 percent of the person's net worth over the same period.

◆ Make the donor's best interests your priority.

◆ Prioritize prospects to spend the most time where you have the greatest potential for major gifts.

◆ Use probing questions to learn what's most important to prospects: "If cost were no object, what would be the ideal solution?" "If we were to establish this program, what should it accomplish?"

◆ If you're hesitant to suggest a specific solicitation amount up front, use a chart that identifies levels of major gifts. Ask the prospect to picture himself among this group of donors.

◆ Never walk away from a rejection without knowing why you were refused. The answer may give clues that will lead to a gift. Answers also help spot trends in your closing method that you should change.

◆ To illustrate donor benefits of particular gift types, share real life examples of how a similar gift is benefiting the donor.

To Recap

The three key ingredients in securing a major gift are the Linkage, Ability, and Interest of the donor. Research will be necessary before making the "ask," and one of the goals of this research is finding the right person to make the "ask." Team solicitations usually work best for major donor prospects.

Plan to conduct screening and strategy meetings with your campaign volunteers to determine who has the best linkage with the prospective donor, what the donor's ability is to give, and how much interest the prospective donor has in specific programs of your organization. During the strategy session you should try to determine if a named giving opportunity is appropriate for this person, and be sure to discuss the various named giving opportunities with the donor.

Always provide training for volunteers and staff who will be contacting donors, whether they will be calling on major donors, or calling donors on the phone to make smaller gifts.

Be sure to ask every prospective donor for a specific amount, and ask for the highest amount you think this prospect is capable of giving.

Chapter Ten

Campaign Events and Public Relations

IN THIS CHAPTER

···→ Can we raise money for our campaign through special events?

···→ What types of events are appropriate during a campaign?

···→ How do we avoid having our staff and volunteers spend an inordinate amount of time planning special events during the campaign?

Some typical events that will take place in the campaign are:

◆ Cultivation Breakfasts, Luncheons, Dinner, Cocktail Parties

◆ Kickoff Event

◆ Ground-breaking Event

◆ Dedication and Open House

While a capital campaign should not depend on events to raise the needed money for the project, events are an important step in the campaign process. Volunteers and donors should be cultivated, inspired, and recognized throughout the process.

important

Cultivation Events

As we discussed in an earlier chapter, many donors need more information before they can make a decision to support the campaign. Often of this cultivation will be one-on-one and will be handled through the solicitation committees. However, it often makes sense to do a series of cultivation events designed to bring in small groups of people, usually with a common interest, to provide information about the project. Some examples of cultivation events are:

◆ A series of "cottage meetings" held by a community library, in which a library volunteer and/or donor invites a group of their friends and neighbors into their home. These meetings would be information sessions where prospective donors can learn more about the library's building plans and the campaign.

◆ A church could hold a series of information meetings, again hosted in the homes of some of their parishioners who will gather to hear from the pastor about the vision for the church and how the campaign will allow the church to achieve its vision.

◆ The board members and campaign cabinet for a human service agency might each invite a dozen or so of their friends to come into the organization's facility for a luncheon at which the Executive Director and campaign chair talk about the campaign and the project.

◆ A group of business people might be invited in for an information breakfast meeting at which your organization's leadership can explain the need for this campaign.

Various media will usually be used at these events to tell the story—posters with architectural drawings, a PowerPoint presentation, an information packet, perhaps even a live preview of the campaign website or a video presentation.

The Kickoff Event

Generally, the key event in a campaign is the kickoff event, which is usually the campaign's major event. The primary focus of the kickoff event is to announce the campaign, but other key components of the event are to recognize donors who have already given and to inspire new donors to the campaign. Kickoff events can range from a formal black tie dinner or a cocktail party, to a series of luncheons in different regions or an outdoor garden party, or even a Bar-B-Q at a ranch.

Regardless of the venue, it is important to remember that the kickoff event should not happen until about 60 to 80 percent of the goal has been raised. Announcing a campaign prematurely can be the "kiss of death" for the campaign. Donors will feel the campaign is not going well and will not reach its goal if it seems too distant. On the other hand, if the goal is too close to being reached, donors will think your organization does not need their pledge, since success is imminent.

important

A tentative event date can be set early on in the campaign planning process, but should be confirmed when it is apparent that the campaign is on track with pledges and gifts. The kickoff event should be included in the campaign budget, as there is usually no charge for attending the event. The plan is to get as many key donors to attend the event as possible. Donors who have already come on board should be recognized at the kickoff, including board, staff, and leadership donors. This sets the pace for future donors to get involved. A poster with all the donor names, listing in the program book, or even unveiling the donor recognition plaque with the leadership donor names already engraved can be inspiring to those who have not yet made their pledge, but want to be included in the campaign and included in the final donor recognition. A large donor might be asked to speak about why he or she has invested in this project. A testimonial by someone who has received services from your organization is also an inspiring way to motivate donors. Whatever type of event you choose, it should always be upbeat and inspirational.

Groundbreaking

The groundbreaking is another event your organization can celebrate. For some organizations, ground isn't broken until the campaign has been completed, and in these cases the groundbreaking and victory celebration can be one and the same. For other organizations, groundbreaking might be done at the kickoff event, or happens during the campaign, and then the dedication and open house become the victory celebration. The timing of the project and the events should be carefully coordinated in the overall campaign calendar. An event committee is responsible for coordinating all the campaign events.

Dedication

You will also want to plan a dedication of the new facility when it is completed. This is a perfect opportunity to thank all the donors and volunteers and enable the donors to see firsthand the fruits of their donations. You will want to confirm that all donor names are spelled correctly, and print a list of all donors in your program book. You should delay the dedication until you can confirm all the names are correct and until you have the named giving recognition plaques or walls in place. You will want to invite media guests, politicians, and other community leaders in addition to all donors and volunteers. Speeches should be kept to a minimum; you should write speeches for donors and volunteers, if possible, to make sure they aren't too lengthy (or too short). You will also want to arrange to have some volunteers or clients lead tours of the facility.

Public Relations for the Campaign

The public relations committee of the campaign cabinet is responsible for all the various public relations for the campaign. These may include:

◆ Campaign theme and logo

◆ Campaign printed materials, including brochures, letterhead and envelopes, response envelopes, letters of intent, fact sheets, and question and answer sheets

◆ Campaign video and/or PowerPoint

◆ Press Releases

◆ Campaign website, which can include a webcam tracking construction progress

◆ Press Conferences

◆ Campaign Speeches

◆ Promotional Items

The PR Committee usually works with the consultant and staff to design the theme and logo. The brochures and other campaign materials are developed based on the case for support and need to be completed early enough that various committees can use them in their work. Like campaign events, it is important not to release information about the campaign too early in the process. Often pre-campaign publicity is planned to focus on the organization's programs and services without mentioning the actual campaign. It simply promotes awareness of the organization so that, when the campaign is launched publicly, there will be sufficient public interest in the project to assure a successful campaign.

To Recap

Events are important aspects of your capital campaign, but should not be relied on to raise money. It will be important to involve volunteers on the campaign cabinet who will handle these events so the staff does not spend all its time planning and managing events.

Typical events during a campaign include cultivation events, the kickoff event, groundbreaking, and a dedication event at the end of the campaign.

Public relations during the campaign remains important but, like events, it must be carefully tied to and worked into the campaign calendar at the appropriate times. It is critical not to "go public" until you've raised 60 to 80 percent of the campaign goal.

Chapter Eleven

Recognition and Stewardship

IN THIS CHAPTER

···→ How do we recognize donors to the capital campaign?

···→ What type of ethical situations might arise during the campaign?

···→ How do we assure that pledges are fulfilled?

I t has been said that good stewardship is the last step in the first gift and the first step in the next gift. Stewardship includes ensuring that the donor's best interests are always the primary consideration, conforming to all applicable laws, making certain that all fundraising is done with the highest ethical standards, and developing proper systems of acknowledgment and recognition for the donor.

Donors should never be persuaded to contribute to a cause they don't fully support, or to make a gift that may not be in their own best interest. The Association of Fundraising Professionals (AFP) provides a code of ethical standards and principles of professional practice that serves as a guide for its members but can provide a solid ethical basis for all fundraisers.

This code may be found in the **Appendix B.** In addition to this code, numerous other professional organizations have similar codes of ethics. Some common issues that appear in all these codes are that fundraisers, either staff or consultants, should never work on a percentage based fee, that fundraisers must be open and honest about the organization and its mission, and that fundraisers will always conform to legal requirements regarding the solicitations, recording, use and acknowledgement of gifts. In addition to these codes of ethics is a Donor Bill of Rights, which may be found in **Appendix C.** This Bill of Rights informs the donor of things they are entitled to when making a gift to a nonprofit. For example, donors have a right to know who is on the governing board of the organization; whether the person soliciting them is a professional counsel, paid staff, or a volunteer; and the right to remain anonymous in their giving among, other things. Organizations and fundraisers should promote this Bill of Rights and adhere to its principles.

Legal Issues

Other important aspects of all fundraising that must be considered during a campaign are the legal requirements of the IRS and other regulatory agencies, such as state and local municipalities that may govern fundraising activities. For example, most states regulate fundraising activities by requiring nonprofit organizations, fundraising counsel, and professional solicitors to register with them before conducting fundraising campaigns. For information on state requirements, contact your department of state.

> You should be aware of your own state's requirements as well as other states in which you may plan to solicit donations. You also need to be sure that, before engaging a paid consultant or professional solicitor, that firm is registered within the state, if required.
>
> **watch out!**

IRS requirements in regard to "quid pro quo" contributions, fair market value of considerations given to donors, and statements for donations over $250 must be followed in the recording and acknowledgment of gifts. The organization's accounting firm can give advice and counsel regarding IRS regulations *(This book is not meant to provide legal or accounting advice. Please contact appropriate counsel for this advice.)*

Acknowledgment of donors' gifts should always be made promptly. Sending a thank you letter within twenty-four hours of receiving a gift is recommended. All donors should be acknowledged with a personal letter of thanks, regardless of the size of their gift.

The Rule of 7

While you would not want to send seven thank-you letters to a donor, there are other ways to say thanks. A personal phone call from the volunteer who solicited the gift, a handwritten note from the executive director or chair of the board, a phone call from a program recipient—all can do wonders to bond the donor to your organization. And, of course, the formal receipt with the IRS-prescribed statement that no goods or services were received in consideration of this donation can be considered another form of thanking the donor.

> It is said that a donor should be thanked seven times for a gift before asking for the next gift.
>
> practical tip

Recognition

Recognition is another facet of thanking the donor for their gift. Recognition can come in many forms. Listing donors in your organization's newsletter and/or annual report, issuing a press release about a major gift, donor walls, bricks, and personal mementos given to the donors are all ways of providing donor recognition. Brick walkways or walls are not only a great way to recognize donors, but serve as an incentive to get smaller donors to give multiple gifts so they (or each member of their family) can have a brick. You can also use various size bricks or stones to commemorate various levels of giving. Although the recognition walls will be installed when the building is completed, you should plan your recognition at the beginning of the campaign so it can be used to leverage gifts.

Special recognition events at which donors are publicly recognized for their contributions can also be effective. Remember, however, that some donors wish to remain anonymous, and their anonymity must always be ensured. Providing a place on the pledge card or letter of intent for donors to print their name exactly the way they wish to be recognized, and a box where they can check if they want to remain anonymous, are simple ways to ensure that recognition will be according to the donor's wishes. A good software system (discussed in an earlier chapter) will provide the means to track this information when it is time to prepare recognition items. Of course, these pledge forms and software systems must be in place at the start of your campaign, so recognition must be considered before the campaign begins and be a part of the campaign plan, not decided at the end of the campaign when it is time to recognize donors.

Besides adhering to legal and ethical standards, you will benefit from good stewardship in other ways, as well. Professional staff will feel more confident knowing they are acting according to the highest professional standards, and donors feel more confident knowing the organizations they support follows good stewardship practices. Many an organization has been the beneficiary of a huge estate, because they provided good stewardship of the donor's smaller gifts.

To Recap

Donor recognition is important and should be planned and budgeted for at the beginning of your campaign. Recognition can be an incentive for some donors to give or to give at a higher level than they may have initially considered. Be sure you allow for donors who want to remain anonymous to do so.

Be aware of federal, state, and local legal requirements before beginning your campaign. Know and adhere to the AFP Code of Ethics and Standards of Practice. And provide the Donor Bill of Rights to your donors.

Chapter Twelve

Life After the Campaign

IN THIS CHAPTER

···➔ How to benefit from the improved infrastructure you've developed during the campaign

···➔ How to build on the relationships you've built with donors and volunteers

···➔ How can the increased publicity gained during the campaign benefit your organization in the long run?

T he campaign is over, and generally the first thing you are probably ready to do after the final campaign celebration is to kick back and relax. A well-deserved vacation, or at least a few days off is probably a good idea. However, before the glow of a successful campaign fades, you should think about how your organization can "capitalize" on its success to build a stronger development program and stronger organization for the future.

One of the major benefits of a successful campaign is that it leaves an organization much stronger than it was prior to the campaign. The reasons for this are several:

◆ The campaign starts with an internal assessment, and from that assessment comes recommendations to strengthen the infrastructure of the organization;

◆ Increased public relations efforts during a campaign results in a heightened awareness of the organization in the community;

◆ Volunteer involvement in the campaign provides future volunteer fundraisers for the organization's ongoing development efforts;

◆ Staff benefits from working with a consultant, and gains knowledge and experience that is an asset to them and the organization.

Systems

The database system developed for the campaign must be maintained on an ongoing basis, and pledge reminders should be sent to ensure a good collection rate on pledges. Donor pledges should be tracked and, when the pledge is paid off, it may be time to invite the donor to increase their annual giving. This may even happen while pledges are being fulfilled. Some organizations fear asking donors for additional funds, but once donors have supported a major project, their level of interest in the organization as well as their level of commitment generally increases dramatically, and they are more likely to support the organization on an ongoing basis. These donors should be included in annual fund appeals as soon as they become part of the database system.

> Soon after the end of a campaign, you should hold a debriefing with the board, staff, and campaign volunteers to discuss what went right, what went wrong, what should be done differently next time, and how to build on this success to enhance the organization's development program.

important

Donors

Staying in touch with donors on a regular basis and keeping them updated on the progress of the campaign and the project are important. Inviting all donors to the dedication and open house when the new facility is completed are steps that sometimes get overlooked. But remember, the key to successful fundraising is relationships, relationships, relationships; so, in order to build these good relationships the organization needs to maintain good donor communication. Be sure to add all donors to your newsletter list, invite them to events, and ask them to support your annual appeal. And, do update donors on what is happening in the building, what programs you've been able to add, how many more people you are able to serve, and how much more efficient you are because of new equipment. Donors want to know how their money was used, and reporting success to them can only result in future gifts when you approach them the next time. Don't forget to send donors a final campaign report with the list of all donors, and put them on the list to receive your annual reports.

Volunteers

Like donors, campaign volunteers will have developed more awareness and commitment to the organization. Keeping campaign volunteers involved in the organization's ongoing development efforts can be a real boost to fundraising. Volunteers can help in the annual fund, major gifts programs, and planned giving campaigns, especially those who have been involved in making personal solicitations. They will have the training to be effective fundraisers, because of their involvement in the campaign. Be sure at the beginning of the campaign that you've established a system to track the success each volunteer has with their donor solicitation. Those who have been the most successful you will want to keep involved in future fundraising efforts, especially your major gifts and planned giving programs. You might also invite some of these volunteers to serve on your board or the development committee.

The Board

The board's role in the campaign may have been the first exposure they have had to the importance of their own giving. This commitment should be built upon in future annual appeals by starting every year's fundraising program with an annual board appeal. Through their involvement in the campaign, Board members, like volunteers, will have more experience in and knowledge about fundraising, so they can now be invited to get more involved in your organization's ongoing development efforts. This is a good time to ensure that board members stay involved in fundraising efforts and continue to help in the process of identifying, cultivating, and soliciting donors. Perhaps some of your board members would like to continue the cultivation activities by agreeing to host a cultivation event once a year. If each board member commits to one cultivation event a year, you will have a never-ending supply of new donor prospects. Board members who have been successful in raising money for the capital campaign might now be willing to serve on the development committee or get more involved in your major gift efforts.

Public Awareness

The increased public awareness of the organization during the campaign can help it tremendously. Continue to cultivate media contacts made during the campaign for their ongoing support of the organization. Getting stories in the newspaper about the increased services the organization is able to provide because of the successful campaign will help in future fundraising efforts. Be sure to maintain regular contacts with the media every time you add a new program, reach a significant milestone, promote staff, and appoint new board members.

Staff

One of the biggest fears of organizations ending a campaign is that they now have experienced and knowledgeable staff members who have been through the campaign process, developed close relationship with donors, and learned from their work with an experienced, knowledgeable consultant. Now, how do they keep those staff people in the organization? Providing opportunities for continued growth is important for staff. Allowing them to expand into new roles within the organization, recognizing them for their efforts during the campaign, and publicly acknowledging their work can all be benefits that can keep staff committed to the organization. Not just development staff should be considered in the growth of an organization. For organizations where there was not a development department in place before the campaign, staff may have been moved from other departments to work on the campaign. If you have not had a development office before, this may be the time to consider having those staff serve permanently in development roles. Or if new staff was hired for the campaign, these new people may be considered for permanent employment in the organization since they now have a commitment to the organization and valuable experience.

For some organizations, a capital campaign may be a once in a lifetime occurrence. For others, they will be ready for another campaign within a few years after the current one ends. Regardless of which situation your organization is in, don't miss out on the opportunity to build a stronger organization after the campaign ends.

Remember that your campaign plan should include some post-campaign steps as well as preparing you for a successful campaign.

If there is one thing I hope you've learned from this book, it is the importance of planning. To help you get started, I've included a planning grid in **Appendix A,** Plan of Action, that can help you plan your campaign from start to finish.

practical tip

To Recap

Life does not end for your organization or your development department once the campaign is ended. Be sure to maintain and build on the relationships you've built during the campaign. Keep volunteers involved. Continue cultivating donors for renewed and increased gifts. Remember to provide good stewardship and uphold high ethical standards. Keep your donor database up to date. Continue public relations efforts. Be certain that your board is involved in ongoing fundraising efforts. Continue educating board, staff and volunteers. And celebrate your success!

Appendix A—Plan of Action

[Worksheet begins on following page]

For the full-sized PDF file of this resource contact the author at:

 http://charitychannel.com/cc/linda-lysakowski

Name: _____ Organization: _____ Date _____

Purpose of Campaign: _____

Monetary Goal of Campaign: _____ Anticipated Start Date of Campaign _____ Ending Date _____

Objective	Tasks	Budget	Due Date	Responsibility	Completed
1. Meet all legal requirements to do fund raising					
2. Obtain necessary approvals for conducting campaign					
3. Obtain board approval of campaign					
4. Appoint a campaign steering committee					
5. Assess internal readiness—conduct development program audits					

Objective	Tasks	Budget	Due Date	Responsibility	Completed
6. Complete site study and preliminary site plan and determine endowment needs					
7. Purchase and install donor software/ hardware					
8. Hire consultant to do planning study					
9. Prepare preliminary case for support					
10. Complete Planning Study					
11. Hire necessary staff to manage campaign operations					
12. Hire consultant for campaign					
13. Prepare campaign timetable, organizational chart and gift table					

Objective	Tasks	Budget	Due Date	Responsibility	Completed
14. Prepare final case for support					
15. Recruit Campaign Cabinet					
16. Prepare public relations plan for campaign					
17. Develop leadership prospect list					
18. Kick off leadership phase of campaign--individuals, corporate, foundation					
19. Prepare campaign materials					
20. Hold Cultivation Events					
21. Complete Leadership phase of campaign					

Objective	Tasks	Budget	Due Date	Responsibility	Completed
22. Hold campaign kickoff event to announce public (general) phase of campaign					
23. Begin General Phase of campaign: Individuals, business organizations					
24. Plan and execute donor recognition program					
25. Complete campaign clean up phase to reach all prospects					
26. Complete final campaign reports					
27. Plan and execute campaign celebration					
28. Debriefing on campaign and plan for future development efforts					

Appendix B—Code of Ethical Principles and Standards

ETHICAL PRINCIPLES Adopted 1964; amended September 2007

The Association of Fundraising Professionals (AFP) exists to foster the development and growth of fundraising professionals and the profession, to promote high ethical behavior in the fundraising profession and to preserve and enhance philanthropy and volunteerism.

Members of AFP are motivated by an inner drive to improve the quality of life through the causes they serve. They serve the ideal of philanthropy, are committed to the preservation and enhancement of volunteerism; and hold stewardship of these concepts as the overriding direction of their professional life. They recognize their responsibility to ensure that needed resources are vigorously and ethically sought and that the intent of the donor is honestly fulfilled.

To these ends, AFP members, both individual and business, embrace certain values that they strive to uphold in performing their responsibilities for generating philanthropic support. AFP business members strive to promote and protect the work and mission of their client organizations.

AFP members both individual and business aspire to:

- Practice their profession with integrity, honesty, truthfulness and adherence to the absolute obligation to safeguard the public trust

- Act according to the highest goals and visions of their organizations, professions, clients and consciences

- Put philanthropic mission above personal gain

- Inspire others through their own sense of dedication and high purpose

- Improve their professional knowledge and skills, so that their performance will better serve others

- Demonstrate concern for the interests and well-being of individuals affected by their actions

- Value the privacy, freedom of choice and interests of all those affected by their actions

- Foster cultural diversity and pluralistic values and treat all people with dignity and respect

- Affirm, through personal giving, a commitment to philanthropy and its role in society

- Adhere to the spirit as well as the letter of all applicable laws and regulations

- Advocate within their organizations adherence to all applicable laws and regulations

- Avoid even the appearance of any criminal offense or professional misconduct

- Bring credit to the fundraising profession by their public demeanor

- Encourage colleagues to embrace and practice these ethical principles and standards

- Be aware of the codes of ethics promulgated by other professional organizations that serve philanthropy

ETHICAL STANDARDS

Furthermore, while striving to act according to the above values, AFP members, both individual and business, agree to abide (and to ensure, to the best of their ability, that all members of their staff abide) by the AFP standards. Violation of the standards might subject the member to disciplinary sanctions, including expulsion, as provided in the AFP Ethics Enforcement Procedures.

Member Obligations

1. Members shall not engage in activities that harm the members' organizations, clients or profession.

2. Members shall not engage in activities that conflict with their fiduciary, ethical and legal obligations to their organizations, clients or profession.

3. Members shall effectively disclose all potential and actual conflicts of interest; such disclosure does not preclude or imply ethical impropriety.

4. Members shall not exploit any relationship with a donor, prospect, volunteer, client or employee for the benefit of the members or the members' organizations.

5. Members shall comply with all applicable local, state, provincial and federal civil and criminal laws.

6. Members recognize their individual boundaries of competence and are forthcoming and truthful about their professional experience and qualifications and will represent their achievements accurately and without exaggeration.

7. Members shall present and supply products and/or services honestly and without misrepresentation and will clearly identify the details of those products, such as availability of the products and/or services and other factors that may affect the suitability of the products and/or services for donors, clients or nonprofit organizations.

8. Members shall establish the nature and purpose of any contractual relationship at the outset and will be responsive and available to organizations and their employing organizations before, during and after any sale of materials and/or services. Members will comply with all fair and reasonable obligations created by the contract.

9. Members shall refrain from knowingly infringing the intellectual property rights of other parties at all times. Members shall address and rectify any inadvertent infringement that may occur.

10. Members shall protect the confidentiality of all privileged information relating to the provider/client relationships.

11. Members shall refrain from any activity designed to disparage competitors untruthfully.

Solicitation and Use of Philanthropic Funds

12. Members shall take care to ensure that all solicitation and communication materials are accurate and correctly reflect their organizations' mission and use of solicited funds.

13. Members shall take care to ensure that donors receive informed, accurate and ethical advice about the value and tax implications of contributions.

14. Members shall take care to ensure that contributions are used in accordance with donors' intentions.

15. Members shall take care to ensure proper stewardship of all revenue sources, including timely reports on the use and management of such funds.

16. Members shall obtain explicit consent by donors before altering the conditions of financial transactions.

Presentation of Information

17. Members shall not disclose privileged or confidential information to unauthorized parties.

18. Members shall adhere to the principle that all donor and prospect information created by, or on behalf of, an organization or a client is the property of that organization or client and shall not be transferred or utilized except on behalf of that organization or client.

19. Members shall give donors and clients the opportunity to have their names removed from lists that are sold to, rented to or exchanged with other organizations.

20. Members shall, when stating fundraising results, use accurate and consistent accounting methods that conform to the appropriate guidelines adopted by the American Institute of Certified Public Accountants (AICPA)* for the type of organization involved. (*In countries outside of the United States, comparable authority should be utilized.)

Compensation and Contracts

21. Members shall not accept compensation or enter into a contract that is based on a percentage of contributions; nor shall members accept finder's fees or contingent fees. Business members must refrain from receiving compensation from third parties derived

from products or services for a client without disclosing that third-party compensation to the client (for example, volume rebates from vendors to business members).

22. Members may accept performance-based compensation, such as bonuses, provided such bonuses are in accord with prevailing practices within the members' own organizations and are not based on a percentage of contributions.

23. Members shall neither offer nor accept payments or special considerations for the purpose of influencing the selection of products or services.

24. Members shall not pay finder's fees, commissions or percentage compensation based on contributions, and shall take care to discourage their organizations from making such payments.

25. Any member receiving funds on behalf of a donor or client must meet the legal requirements for the disbursement of those funds. Any interest or income earned on the funds should be fully disclosed.

Appendix C—Donor Bill of Rights

Philanthropy is based on voluntary action for the common good. It is a tradition of giving and sharing that is primary to the quality of life. To assure that philanthropy merits the respect and trust of the general public, and that donors and prospective donors can have full confidence in the nonprofit organizations and causes they are asked to support, we declare that all donors have these rights:

I
To be informed of the organization's mission, of the way the organization intends to use donated resources, and of its capacity to use donations effectively for their intended purposes.

II
To be informed of the identity of those serving on the organization's governing board, and to expect the board to exercise prudent judgment in its stewardship responsibilities.

III
To have access to the organization's most recent financial statements.

IV
To be assured their gifts will be used for the purposes for which they were given.

V

To receive appropriate acknowledgment and recognition.

VI

To be assured that information about their donations is handled with respect and with confidentiality to the extent provided by law.

VII

To expect that all relationships with individuals representing organizations of interest to the donor will be professional in nature.

VIII

To be informed whether those seeking donations are volunteers, employees of the organization or hired solicitors.

IX

To have the opportunity for their names to be deleted from mailing lists that an organization may intend to share.

X

To feel free to ask questions when making a donation and to receive prompt, truthful and forthright answers.

The text of this statement in its entirety was developed by the American Association of Fund-Raising Counsel (AAFRC), Association for Healthcare Philanthropy (AHP), Council for Advancement and Support of Education (CASE), and the Association of Fundraising Professionals (AFP), and adopted in November 1993.

Appendix D—Suggested Reading

Dove, Kent E.: *Conducting a Successful Capital Campaign,* Jossey-Bass, San Francisco, 1988

Fredricks, Laura: *The ASK: How to Ask for your Nonprofit Cause, Creative Project, or Business Venture,* Jossey-Bass, San Francisco, 2010

Lysakowski, Linda: *Recruiting and Training Fundraising Volunteers,* Wiley & Sons, New York, 2005

Stroman, M. Kent: *Asking about Asking: Mastering the Art of Conversational Fundraising,* CharityChannel Press, Rancho Santa Margarita, 2011

Seiler, Timothy: *Developing Your Case for Support,* Jossey-Bass, San Francisco, 2001

Appendix E—Campaign Assignments Worksheet

[Worksheet starts on following page]

_____

For the full-sized PDF file of this resource contact the author at:

 http://charitychannel.com/cc/linda-lysakowski

Activities	Skills Needed	Who in Our Organization Can do this Activity?	Do We Need to Hire Consultant or Staff member for this Activity?
Organize/define campaign goals and objectives	◆ Management and planning skills ◆ Knowledge of community needs ◆ Knowledge of organization's needs		
Organize/prepare schedules and guidelines	◆ Management/planning skills ◆ Budgeting skills ◆ Fundraising experience ◆ Campaign experience		

Activities	Skills Needed	Who in Our Organization Can do this Activity?	Do We Need to Hire Consultant or Staff member for this Activity?
Write Case Statement	◆ Knowledge of organization ◆ Knowledge of the project ◆ Writing skills ◆ Understanding the psychology of philanthropy ◆ Knowledge of fundraising techniques		
Write and distribute campaign literature	◆ Writing skills ◆ Knowledge of graphics/printing ◆ Direct/bulk mail experience ◆ Marketing skills		

Activities	Skills Needed	Who in Our Organization Can do this Activity?	Do We Need to Hire Consultant or Staff member for this Activity?
Recruit, train, and motivate volunteers	◆ Community contacts ◆ Leadership qualities ◆ Previous experience working with volunteers ◆ Group motivation experience ◆ Education training ◆ Knowledge of fundraising techniques		

Activities	Skills Needed	Who in Our Organization Can do this Activity?	Do We Need to Hire Consultant or Staff member for this Activity?
Solicit prospects	◆ Knowledge of the community ◆ Communication skills ◆ Understanding of the psychology of philanthropy ◆ Financial commitment to campaign		
Keep records and write reports	◆ Administrative skills ◆ Knowledge of campaign software ◆ Accounting skills ◆ Writing skills		
Handle campaign publicity	◆ Understanding of media requirements ◆ Communication skills ◆ Organizational/planning skills		

Appendix F—Sample Preliminary Case Statement

ABC Theatre Association
"Preserving a Treasure"

Case for Support

OUR MISSION

The ABC Theatre Association, a nonprofit, volunteer organization, is committed to preserving and operating a quality performing arts facility in both a fiscally and socially responsible manner to further develop the civic, cultural, and artistic needs of the ABC regional community.

OUR VISION

The proposed adaptive reuse of the ABC Theatre as a performing arts center will be unique among cultural institutions by virtue of its program diversity. It will serve as a combination theatrical stage, concert hall, dance studio, movie cinema, community center, and meeting place.

OUR GOALS

The new ABC Theatre will provide:

1. Special events of interest to residents of ABC County and audiences of the greater ABC region;

2. Repertory presentations of films not presented by commercial theatres in ABC County;

3. Professional cultural programs for children and adults not currently held in ABC County because a suitable facility does not currently exist;

4. Opportunities for community performing arts development;

5. Rental opportunities for local businesses and organizations.

ABOUT THE ABC THEATRE ASSOCIATION

In 1995 a regional plan identified a performing arts center as essential for the XYZ of XYZ's further evolution into a thriving and vibrant community. The ABC Theatre Association (ABC) was created in 1998 to champion the revitalization of the 1910 ABC Theatre located at 123 ABC Street in XYZ, STATE, into a state-of-the-art all-purpose facility for the performing arts. Serving the ABC County Community, the ABC Theatre would provide space for exhibits, theatre, music, and motion picture presentations.

The ABC Theatre Association is working in conjunction with XYZ to bring about the reality of opening the ABC Theatre to the public by late 2002. XYZ purchased the ABC Theatre structure in order to ensure its preservation and continued presence in the community. XYZ also provides administrative support for the project, such as distributing mailings, bookkeeping, and providing a meeting space for XYZ. The partnership between XYZ and ABC is dynamic and allows each organization to perform the activities that best take advantage of their inherent talents and resources.

THE COMMUNITY NEED

The ABC Theatre is an ABC County treasure. Its character-defining features remain intact from its prominent days from 1910-1930 as a reverse screen vaudeville theatre. An early design by noted architect and theatre designer NAME, the restored ABC Theatre will serve the community as it did in the past.

Every community needs art and culture in order to enrich the lives of its residents and help attract new businesses and individuals into the community. A performing arts center is needed in ABC County to compliment the other cultural organizations in the county. Currently, there is no facility like the ABC Theatre in ABC County, a region historically suffering from high rates of out migration of educated younger workers. The ABC Theatre project combines the need for both community and economic development in the ABC County area.

OUR PLAN

The refurbished ABC Theatre will be suitable for many kinds of performances, including plays, musicals, theatre, dance, concerts, and movies. The programming developed by XYZ will provide the local community affordable musical and artistic entertainment, a market that arts and culture programs have traditionally ignored. Additionally, the Theatre will be available for use as a meeting place for the multitude of nonprofit and community groups in the area. A number of long established ABC County regional performing arts companies and groups have already expressed an interest in using the Theatre upon its completion, and at least three wish to make the ABC Theatre their permanent home for performances. This mix of resident companies represents a viable year-round program for the Theatre. The Theatre will also serve as a gallery for local artwork, such as painting and sculpture. Public parking is available within 150 feet of the theatre, providing easy access for patrons.

XYZ and ABC have already taken initial steps to ensure the success of the ABC Theatre project. We have installed a new roof on the structure to prevent further deterioration before restoration is complete. Also, cultural resource specialists have already surveyed the building's existing conditions and have made recommendations for its restoration. Last fall, The ABC Theatre was successful in obtaining an unprecedented $100,000 grant from the STATE Historic Museum Commission to complete Phase I of the restoration project. Work in this phase addresses conditions that require immediate intervention and temporary stabilization to mitigate further deterioration of the building. To launch the project and build public interest and enthusiasm, the existing veneer on the façade of the building will be removed, exposing the decorative metal façade underneath, which will be repainted using the original color scheme.

This campaign will enable us to launch Phase II of the project, which will include complete restoration and refurbishment of interior spaces and the exterior. In addition to actual restoration work, the ABC Theatre will require contemporary infrastructure, including signage and illumination, box office services, patron circulation and amenities, and administration space. The plan also includes modern technology, backstage services, loading, storage, scenery preparation, and dressing room facilities, all of which will need to meet the needs of the groups that will use the Theatre.

A capital campaign, which has been approved by the ABC County Capital Campaign Review Board, will provide funding for the Phase II renovation of the Theatre and start-up costs for the performing arts center. Included in these costs are:

Site Work	$20,000
Concrete	42,000
Metal Restoration	16,000
Carpentry	74,000
Thermal & Moisture Protection	20,000
Doors and Windows Repair & Restoration	5,000
Finishes	22,000
Mechanical Systems (Plumbing, Fire Protection, HVAC)	35,000
Electrical Systems	30,000
Stage Equipment	21,000
Seating	30,000
Furniture & Equipment	40,000
Campaign Expenses	45,000
Endowment	85,000
Campaign Total	**$485,000**

OPPORTUNITIES FOR PARTICIPATION:

As with any campaign of this size, it will be crucial to our success to secure gifts from those who are capable of making leadership gifts to the campaign. The following chart is an example of the size gifts needed to ensure successful completion of this project.

Number of Gifts	Giving Society	In the Range of	For a Total of
1	ABC Circle	$50,000	$50,000
2	Visionary Circle	30,000	110,000
5	Founder's Circle	15,000	185,000
10	Leadership Circle	10,000	285,000
15	Benefactors	6,000	375,000
20	Patrons	3,000	435,000
Many	Friends	Under 3,000	485,000

We will seek three-year pledges from individuals, businesses, and foundations throughout ABC County who are interested in preserving this important part of our cultural heritage.

Within the campaign will be numerous opportunities to name an area of the Theatre in memory of a loved one, or in honor of your family or your company. Among the named giving opportunities will be:

Naming of Theatre	**$250,000**
Lobby	50,000
Reception Area	50,000
Stage	30,000
Orchestra Pit	30,000
Box Office	15,000
Projection Room	15,000
Dressing Rooms (2)	15,000 each
All Purpose Room	15,000
Decorative Windows (14)	10,000 each
Manager's Office	10,000
Stage Manager's Office	10,000

Decorative Ceiling Medallions (5)	10,000 each
Decorative Columns (16)	5,000 each
Seats (approximately 200)	500 each

EXECUTIVE COMMITTEE

NAME   NAME

NAME   NAME

NAME   NAME

NAME   NAME

NAME   NAME

NAME   NAME

CAMPAIGN CABINET

NAME, Honorary Chair

NAME, Chair

NAME, XYZ Business Association

NAME, ABC County Chamber of Commerce

NAME, Co-Chair Major Gifts

NAME, Co-Chair Leadership Gifts

NAME, Co-Chair Phonathon

NAME, Co-Chair, Publicity

NAME, Co-Chair Special Events

NAME, Co-Chair Leadership Gifts

NAME, XYZ

NAME, Co-Chair Small Business Gifts

NAME, Co-Chair Phonathon

NAME, Co-Chair Small Business Gifts

NAME, Co-Chair Publicity

NAME, Co-Chair Special Events

NAME, Chair Board Appeal

NAME, Chair XYZ Board Appeal

NAME, Co-Chair Major Gifts

NAME, Campaign Counsel

Appendix G—Sample of a Compelling Emotional Statement from a Case for Support

A Residential Success Story

John has a smile that can light up a room. On Tuesday, May 8, 2001 the native of our city did just that as he accepted a Community Star Award from the State Association of Community Providers during the organization's annual banquet.

Our staff nominated John because of his outstanding accomplishments in the twenty-five years that he has been affiliated with our agency.

"We are so proud of John. We have pictures of him playing with his buddies in our summer camp from the late '70s. It is great to see how far he has come," said the ABC organization executive director.

John lived at home with his mother Mary and his father Joe until he was accepted at the XYZ School. When he graduated, he returned to ABC County and moved into our Group Home in XYZ Township in 1985. In the early 1990s, John lived in the XYC Supervised Apartments in XYZ, and then, while remaining in his apartment, took the next step towards greater independence and began to receive assistance only several times a week through the agency's Supported Living Program.

On August 28, 1997, John took a huge step and, with the support of his family and The XYZ, purchased his own home. In the agency video, John looks into the camera and states that home ownership is "just peachy."

John's townhouse is lovely, and he likes living there. According to Sally, John's Supported Living Counselor, new furniture, in particular a swivel chair, will make his house a real show-stopper.

A nine-year employee of the ABC Hotel housekeeping department, he works swing shift and, by all accounts, is a hard and dedicated worker. He recently summed up his sentiment for his job by saying, rather unequivocally, "I will work until retirement. I will never leave. My job is good."

His mother and father are so proud of their eldest child. "I just can't tell you how blessed we are. He really has come so far," Mrs. Smith said in a recent conversation. "Please, let everyone know that my husband and I both feel so grateful."

Appendix H—Sample Emotional/Rational Appeal as Part of the Case

Our Community & the Arts

Are the Arts Important?

Many people feel that, with all the human service needs facing our community, the arts are secondary in their contribution to society. Contrary to this belief, consider these facts:

◆ The arts are important to inspiring creativity in our youth;

◆ The arts give people beauty, humor, and a better understanding of different cultures;

◆ The arts are an economic boon to our community.

We would like to give you some food for thought: The United States is no longer a country that produces things, but one that produces ideas. Without the arts, how will our young people be inspired to become the creative, out-of-the-box thinkers on which the future of our country hinges?

To support this premise, in 2005, the opinion research firm Belden, Russonello & Stewart conducted a national poll, in consultation with Douglas Gould & Company. The report of this survey is entitled, "To Educate the Whole Child, Integrate the Arts." The survey sampled 1068 Americans, age eighteen and over, including an over-sample of

152 parents of K-12 students. Some of the surprising data uncovered during this study included these facts:

◆ 48 percent of the American public says there is too little emphasis of arts and music at the elementary school level.

◆ 36 percent of the American public says there is too little emphasis of arts and music at the high school level.

◆ On a scale of one to ten, arts and music as a high priority for public schools rate a seven through ten by 60 percent of the public.

◆ Arts and music are given a higher priority in public schools than standardized tests (56 percent), athletics (52 percent) and foreign languages (48 percent).

◆ 41 percent of Americans say that arts integration is valuable because it educates the whole child.

◆ 22 percent say arts integration is valuable because it inspires creativity.

What do the Arts do for Communities?

The Americans for the Arts conducted a study that shows for every dollar spent on a theater production, the economic impact of that dollar amounts to $27.79 invested in the community (dinner, babysitters, parking, etc.). Another study conducted by the Pew Charitable Trust shows that, when companies are planning to relocate to a new community, they cite the three most important cultural criteria in selecting a location are:

1. Local Community Programs

2. Movies

3. Theater

Appendix I—Checklist for Case Statement Evaluation Worksheet

Look for the feedback in the following area:

❏ Does it elicit emotional as well as rational "reasons" to give?

❏ Does it tell your potential donors how their gift will make a difference?

❏ Does it evoke a sense of the history and long-term importance of your organization and its work?

❏ Does it offer proof that your plan will work?

❏ Are the benefits to the donor clearly stated?

❏ If you include graphs or charts, are they striking?

❏ Is it concise?

❏ Is it reader oriented rather than organization oriented?

❏ Does it emphasize "opportunity" for the donor rather than "need" of the organization?

❏ Is the information presented in a logical order?

❏ Is it readable with short sentences and paragraphs?

❑ Is the typeface appropriate to your organization's appeal?

❑ Is there enough blank space to make it easy to read?

❑ Is the type large enough for reading by older prospects?

❑ Is the cover "striking?"

❑ Is the paper stock attractive without looking expensive?

❑ If you use photographs, are they effective and cropped to maximize impact? (Photos should not include more than two to three people. Large group shots lose dramatic impact.)

———————————————

For the full-sized PDF file of this resource contact the author at:

 http://charitychannel.com/cc/linda-lysakowski

Appendix J—Named Gift Table Worksheet

XYZ ORGANIZATION

"Campaign Theme" Capital Campaign

Named Giving Opportunities

As of MM/DD/YYYY

Named Giving Opportunity	Number Available	Investment Level	Status (available or taken)

◆ Donors of named gifts will have plaques with their names placed in the area named.

◆ Donors of $xxxx or more will be listed on plaque in XYZ lobby.

For the full-sized PDF file of this resource contact the author at:

 http://charitychannel.com/cc/linda-lysakowski

Appendix K—Campaign Materials Worksheet

Type of Campaign:_____

Campaign Goal: _____

Campaign Theme: _____

Number of Constituents: _____

Budget: _____

[Worksheet continues on following pages of this Appendix.]

_____

For the full-sized PDF file of this resource contact the author at:

 http://charitychannel.com/cc/linda-lysakowski

Item	Need	Received	Quantity	Stock	Ink	Size	Design	Printed
Brochure	Case							
	Photos							
	Logo							
	Hours							
	Address/Phone							
	Board							
	Cabinet							

Item	Need	Received	Quantity	Stock	Ink	Size	Design	Printed
	State Registration Information							
Brochure	Indicia							
Envelope	Return Address							
	Logo							
Fact Sheet	Hours							
	Fees							
	Program							

Item	Need	Received	Quantity	Stock	Ink	Size	Design	Printed
	Budget							
Pledge Card	Giving Levels							
	Named Gifts							
	Match Gift Ask							
	State Registration Information							
Letter of Intent	Giving Levels							
	Named Gifts							

Item	Need	Received	Quantity	Stock	Ink	Size	Design	Printed
	Chair							
	State Registration Information							
	Logo							
Levels of Giving	Levels							
	Payment Options							
Named Gift Chart	Named Gifts							
Response Envelope	Giving Levels							

Item	Need	Received	Quantity	Stock	Ink	Size	Design	Printed
	Named Gifts							
	Planned Giving							
	Volunteer Opportunities							
Sponsor	Sponsor Opportunities							
Letterhead	Director List							
	Cabinet							
	Logo							

Item	Need	Received	Quantity	Stock	Ink	Size	Design	Printed
	State Registration Information							
#10 Env	Return Address							
	Indicia							
Other								

Appendix L—Sample Table of Gifts Chart

XYZ ORGANIZATION

Campaign Title Capital Campaign

Goal $2,000,000

Giving Cat-egory	Invest-ment Level	Number of Gifts Needed	Number of Pros-pects Required	Total Dollars in This Level	Cumula-tive Total	Percent of Goal
Leader-ship Gifts	$200,000	1	3	$200,000	$200,000	10%
Leader-ship Gifts	$100,000	1	3	$100,000	$300,000	15%
Major Gifts	$75,000	4	12	$300,000	$600,000	30%
Major Gifts	$50,000	6	18	$300,000	$900,000	45%
Major Gifts	$25,000	10	30	$250,000	$1,150,000	58%

Giving Category	Investment Level	Number of Gifts Needed	Number of Prospects Required	Total Dollars in This Level	Cumulative Total	Percent of Goal
Special Gifts	$20,000	12	36	$240,000	$1,390,000	70%
Special Gifts	$15,000	14	42	$210,000	$1,600,000	80%
Special Gifts	$10,000	16	48	$160,000	$1,760,000	88%
Support Gifts	$5,000	22	66	$110,000	$1,870,000	93%
Support Gifts	$2,500	32	96	$80,000	$1,950,000	97%
Support Gifts	$1,000	50	150	$50,000	$2,000,000	100%
Totals		168	504		$2.000,000	100%

For the full-sized PDF file of this resource contact the author at:

 http://charitychannel.com/cc/linda-lysakowski

Appendix M—Sample Questions Asked During Planning Study Interviews

1. Interviewee's perception of XYZ:

   ☐ Excellent   ☐   Good   ☐ Average   ☐ Poor   ☐ Unaware

   Comments:

   _____

2. Interviewee's understanding of the needs of XYZ:

   ☐ Good   ☐ Poor

   Comments:

   _____

3. How would you prioritize the needs of XYZ?

   a. _____

   b. _____

   c._____

4. Interviewee's acceptance of the plan:

    ☐ Right Plan   ☐ Wrong Plan

    Comments:

    _____

5. Interviewee's approval of campaign:

    ☐ Yes   ☐ No

    Comments:

    _____

6. Is goal attainable?

    ☐ Yes   ☐ No   If no, suggest goal _____

7. Is top gift available?

    ☐ Yes   ☐ No   If no, suggest amt. _____

8. Timing of Campaign:

    ☐ Good   ☐ Not Good   If not good, suggest time _____

9. CITY's economic outlook:

    ☐ Excellent   ☐ Good   ☐ Average   ☐ Poor

10. XYZ board's fund raising strength:

    ☐ Excellent   ☐ Good   ☐ Average   ☐ Poor

11. What is priority of this campaign in relationship to interviewee's personal philanthropic goals?

    ☐ High   ☐ Medium   ☐ Low   ☐ Nonexistent

12. What is the likelihood of the interviewee making a gift?

    ☐ Lead Gift   ☐ Top 10   ☐ Next 20   ☐ Other   ☐ None

    Where on the scale of gifts might the interviewee's personal gift fall?
    $ _____

13. What is the likelihood of the interviewee's corporate gift?

    ☐ Lead Gift   ☐ Top 10   ☐ Next 20   ☐ Other   ☐ None

    Where on the scale of gifts might the interviewee's corporate gift fall?
    $ _____

14. Is interviewee decision maker for corporate gift?

    ☐ Yes   ☐ No   ☐ If no, who_____

    Corporate areas of interest: _____

15. What are the chances of the interviewee's involvement in the campaign?

    ☐ Leadership   ☐ Somewhat involved   ☐ Not involved

16. Suggestions for top 10 donors:

Name: _____ Amount $_____

Name: _____ Amount $_____

Name: _____ Amount $_____

Name: _____ Amount $_____

Name: _____ Amount $_____

Name: _____ Amount $_____

17. Leadership suggestions:

Name: _____ Position: _____

Accepted? (Yes or No) _____

Name: _____ Position: _____

Accepted? (Yes or No) _____

Name: _____ Position: _____

Accepted? (Yes or No) _____

Name: _____ Position: _____

Accepted? (Yes or No) _____

Name: _____ Position: _____

Accepted? (Yes or No) _____

18. Direct quotes from interviewee:

_____

_____

_____

Appendix N—Sample Table of Contents of a Study Report

TABLE OF CONTENTS

Appendix O—Sample Qualitative and Quantitative Comments from a Study Report

Is the $10,000,000 Goal attainable?

Yes	51	85.00%
No	2	3.33%
Not Sure	7	11.67%

If not, suggested goal:

$25,000,000 – 50,000,000 (1)

$20,000,000 (2)

$8,000,000 (1)

$5,000,000 (1)

Comments regarding goal:

◆ The goal should be much higher. (2)

◆ $7,000,000 is "peanuts" for a scholarship endowment.

◆ They probably need more! $20M is probably not too much.

◆ My first thoughts when I read this were: 1) they could raise a lot more; and, 2) it should only be a three-year campaign; five years is too long, however they could have five years to pay the pledge.

◆ More money is needed; you won't know how much you can raise until you try.

◆ The alumni really care about the school and will support it.

◆ We need to set the bar high; anything is possible if we work hard at it.

Appendix P—Sample Volunteer Plan

CAMPAIGN VOLUNTEER POSITIONS

Committee	Positions	Number of Volunteers
Capital Campaign Cabinet	Chair	1
	Honorary Chair	1
	Chairs and Co-chairs of Committees	14-28
Board Gifts	Chair or Co-Chairs	2
	Members	2-6
Staff Gifts	Chair or Co-Chairs	1-2
	Summer Staff Committee Members	3
Prospect Development & Evaluation	Co-Chairs	2
Leadership Gifts	Co-Chairs	2
	Committee Members	2-4

Major Gifts	Co-Chairs	2
	Vice Chairs	4
	Members	8-12
Special Gifts	Co-Chairs	2
	Vice Chairs	4
	Members	15-20
Vendor & Business	Co-Chairs	2
	Vice-Chairs	4
	Members	15-20
Retired & Current Ministers	Co-Chairs	2
	Region Vice Chairs	4
	Members	8-10
Church Gifts	Co-Chairs	2
	Region Vice Chairs	4
	Members	8-12
Organizations	Co-Chairs	2
	Members	2-3

	Co-Chairs	2
	Region Vice-Chairs	4
	Region Kick Off Event Co-Chairs	4-8
	Region Kick Off Event Committee	4
Special Events	Region Cultivation Events Co-Chairs	4-8
	Region Cultivation Events Committee	20-30
	Dedication Event Co-Chairs	2
	Dedication Event Committee	5-7
	Co-Chairs	2
	Region Vice-Chairs	4
Prayer	Prayer Captains	55
	Committee Members	110-275
Public Relations	Co-Chairs	2
Speakers' Bureau	Co-Chairs	2
Total Volunteers Needed		351-590

For the full-sized PDF file of this resource contact the author at:

 http://charitychannel.com/cc/linda-lysakowski

Appendix Q—Sample Breakdown of Scale of Gifts by Division

Scale of Gifts for $2,800,000 Campaign Goal

Committee	Number of prospects needed	Number of gifts needed	At the following levels	Total
Lead Gifts	3	1	$250,000	$ 250,000
	6	2	150,000	300,000
	15	3	100,000	300,000
Major Gifts	15	5	75,000	375,000
	21	7	50,000	350,000
	30	10	25,000	250,000
Special Gifts	36	12	15,000	180,000
	45	15	10,000	150,000
From a combination of other categories	Many	Many	Under $10,000	645,000
Total				$2,800,000

_____

For the full-sized PDF file of this resource contact the author at:

 http://charitychannel.com/cc/linda-lysakowski

Appendix R—Sample Breakdown of Campaign Elements

Board Gifts
Proposed Goal: $40,000
Gift Range: $500-$9,999

Staff Gifts
Proposed Goal: $20,000
Gift Range: $500-$9,999

Leadership Gifts
Proposed Goal: $850,000
Gift Range: $100,000 and higher

Major Gifts
Proposed Goal: $975,000
Gift Range: $25,000-$99,999

Special Gifts
Proposed Goal: $330,000
Gift Range: $10,000-$24,999

Vendor & Business Gifts
Proposed Goal: $45,000
Gift Range: $1,000-$9,999

Organization Gifts
Proposed Goal: $40,000
Gift Range: $500-$9,999

Retired and Current Minister Gifts
Proposed Goal: $50,000
Gift Range: $1,000-$9,999

Church Gifts
Proposed Goal: $300,000
Gift Range: $1,000-$9,999

Foundation Gifts
Proposed Goal: $150,000
Gift Range: $5,000-$25,000

For the full-sized PDF file of this resource contact the author at:

 http://charitychannel.com/cc/linda-lysakowski

Appendix S—Full Campaign Timeline

Task	Responsibility	Date to Accomplish
Recruit Board Appeal Committee	Board Gifts Chair	September 2008
Prepare Board Solicitation packets	Campaign Counsel; Campaign Coordinator	September 2008
Board "Cast the Vision" Meeting	Executive Director, Board Chair	September 2008
Evaluate staff	Executive Director, Board Chair	September 2008
Appoint Honorary Chair and Vice Chair	Campaign Chair, Campaign Manager, Executive Director	October 2008
Conduct Board Appeal Strategy Session	Campaign Chair, Board Appeal Chair, Executive Director, Campaign Manager, Campaign Counsel	October 2008

Task	Responsibility	Date to Accomplish
Conduct Staff Kickoff Event	Executive Director	October 2008
Develop Preliminary Foundation Gift Prospect List	Campaign Director; Campaign Counsel	October 2008
Solicit Board Member Commitments	Board Appeal Committee	October – November 2008
Solicit Staff	Executive Director	November 2008
Screen Foundation Gift Prospects	Campaign Manager; Campaign Counsel; Board	November 2008
Prepare Final Case for Support	Campaign Counsel, PR Committee	November 2008
Prepare Campaign Budget	Campaign Counsel, Finance Committee	November 2008
Prepare Gift Acceptance Policies	Campaign Manager, Campaign Counsel	November 2008
Appoint Leadership Gifts Co-chairs	Campaign Chair, Vice Chair, Campaign Manager, Executive Director	December 2008
Appoint Major Gifts Co-chairs	Campaign Chair, Vice Chair, Campaign Manager, Executive Director	December 2008
Appoint Special Gifts Co-chairs	Campaign Chair, Vice Chair, Campaign Manager, Executive Director	December 2008
Appoint Small Business Co-chairs	Campaign Chair, Vice Chair, Campaign Manager, Executive Director	December 2008

Task	Responsibility	Date to Accomplish
Appoint Organization Co-chairs	Campaign Chair, Vice Chair, Campaign Manager, Executive Director	December 2008
Recruit Foundation Gifts Committee	Campaign Chair, Vice Chair, Campaign Manager	December 2008
Develop Insider Newsletter	PR Committee/Counsel	December 2008
Follow up to Board if needed	Board Chair	December 2008
Recruit Organization Gifts Committee	Organization Gifts Co-chairs	January 2009
Recruit Leadership Gifts Committee	Leadership Gifts Chairs, Campaign Cabinet	January 2009
Prepare Leadership Gift Prospect List	Prospect Development & Evaluation Committee; Lead Gifts Chair(s); Campaign Manager; Campaign Counsel	January 2009
Distribute Insider Newsletter	PR Committee/Staff	January 2009
Hold Cultivation Events	Cultivation Events Committee	January 2009 – December 2009
Prepare Letters of Inquiry/Proposals to Potential Grant Funders	Campaign Coordinator; Campaign Manager; Campaign Counsel	January 2009 and ongoing
Leadership Gifts Evaluation and Assignment	Leadership Gifts Committee	February 2009

Task	Responsibility	Date to Accomplish
Develop Organizational Gifts Preliminary Prospect List	Organization Gifts Co-Chairs; Campaign Manager; Campaign Counsel	February 2009
Prepare Leadership Gift Materials	Campaign Coordinator; Campaign Counsel	February 2009
Send proposals to foundations at appropriate times	Campaign Manager; Campaign Coordinator	February 2009 and ongoing
Conduct Leadership Gifts Committee Volunteer Strategy & Training	Campaign Counsel	March 2009
Screen Organizational Gift Prospects	Organizations Gifts Co-Chairs; Committee Members	March 2009
Make initial contact with these organizations	Organization Gifts Co-Chairs; Committee Members	March 2009
Conduct Leadership Gifts Solicitation	Leadership Gifts Committee	March 2009 - December 2009
Develop campaign brochures & other printed materials	PR Committee/Counsel	March 2009
Develop PPT/DVD	PR Committee/Counsel	March 2009
Develop Campaign Website Page	PR Committee	March 2009
Hold Foundation Gifts Report Meetings	Campaign Manager; Campaign Counsel	March 2009 and ongoing
Campaign Materials Printed	PR Committee	April 2009

Task	Responsibility	Date to Accomplish
Develop Campaign Newsletter	PR Committee	April 2009
Hold Lead Gift Report Meetings	Leadership Gifts Committee; Campaign Chair; Executive Director; Campaign Director; Campaign Counsel	April 2009 – January 2010
Schedule presentations to organizations or make request for donations	Organization Gifts Co-Chairs; Committee Members	April 2009 and ongoing
Hold Organizational Gifts Report Meetings	Organization Gifts Committee; Campaign Manager; Campaign Counsel	May 2009 and ongoing
Publish Campaign Newsletter	PR Committee Campaign Coordinator	May 2009 and ongoing
Recruit Major Gifts Committee	Major Gifts Co-Chairs	June 2009
Prepare Major Gifts Materials	Campaign Coordinator; Campaign Counsel	July 2009
Identify Major Gifts Prospects	Prospect Development & Evaluation Committee; Major Gifts Co-Chairs; Campaign Manager; Campaign Counsel	July 2009
Recruit Small Business Committee	Small Business Co-Chairs	July 2009
Develop Preliminary Small Business Prospect List	Small Business Co-Chairs; Campaign Director; Campaign Counsel	July 2009

Task	Responsibility	Date to Accomplish
Conduct Major Gifts Evaluation and Assignment Meeting	Major Gifts Committee; Campaign Chair; Executive Director; Campaign Manager; Campaign Counsel	July 2009
Recruit Special Gifts Committee	Special Gifts Co-Chairs	July – August 2009
Prepare Special Gifts Materials	Campaign Coordinator; Campaign Counsel	August 2009
Identify Special Gifts Prospects	Prospect Development & Evaluation Committee, Special Gifts Co-Chairs, Campaign Manager, Campaign Counsel	August 2009
Conduct Special Gift Evaluation and Assignment Meeting	Special Gifts Committee; Campaign Chair; Executive Director; Campaign Manager; Campaign Counsel	August 2009
Conduct Special Gift Evaluation and Assignment Meeting	Special Gifts Committee; Campaign Chair; Executive Director; Campaign Manager; Campaign Counsel	August 2009
Screen Small Business Prospects	Small Business Co-Chairs; Committee Members	August 2009
Prepare Small Business Materials	Campaign Coordinator; Campaign Counsel	August 2009
Conduct Major Gifts Kickoff Meeting	Major Gifts Committee; Campaign Chair; Executive Manager Director; Campaign Counsel	September 2009

Task	Responsibility	Date to Accomplish
Conduct Small Business Solicitations	Small Business Committee	September 2009 – April 2010
Hold Special Gifts Kickoff Meeting	Special Gifts Committee; Campaign Chair; Executive Director; Campaign Manager; Campaign Counsel	September 2009
Hold Small Business Kickoff Meeting	Campaign Chair; Small Business Co-Chairs; Small Business Committee Members; Executive Director; Campaign Manager; Campaign Counsel	September 2009
Hold Kickoff Event	Kickoff Event Committee	October 2009
Conduct Major Gifts Solicitations	Major Gifts Committee	October 2009 – January 2010
Hold Major Gifts Report Meetings	Major Gifts Committee; Campaign Chair; Executive Director; Campaign Manager; Campaign Counsel	November 2009 – February 2010
Conduct Special Gifts Solicitations	Special Gifts Committee	October 2009 – February 2010
Conduct Small Business Solicitations	Special Gifts Committee	October 2009 – February 2010
Hold Special Gifts Report Meetings	Special Gifts Committee; Campaign Chair; Executive Director; Campaign Manager; Campaign Counsel	November 2009 – March 2010

Task	Responsibility	Date to Accomplish
Hold Small Business Gift Report Meetings	Small Business Co-Chairs; Small Business Vice Chairs; Team Leaders; Campaign Manager; Campaign Counsel	November 2009 – March 2010
Identify Direct Mail Prospects	Campaign Cabinet	July 2010
Prepare Direct Mail Materials	Campaign Coordinator; Campaign Manager; Campaign Counsel	August 2010
Conduct Direct Mail Appeal	Campaign Coordinator; Direct Mail Volunteers	September 2010
Hold Dedication Event	Dedication Event Committee	TBD

For the full-sized PDF file of this resource contact the author at:

 http://charitychannel.com/cc/linda-lysakowski

Appendix T—Sample Campaign Organization Chart

[Following page]

For the full-sized PDF file of this resource contact the author at:

 http://charitychannel.com/cc/linda-lysakowski

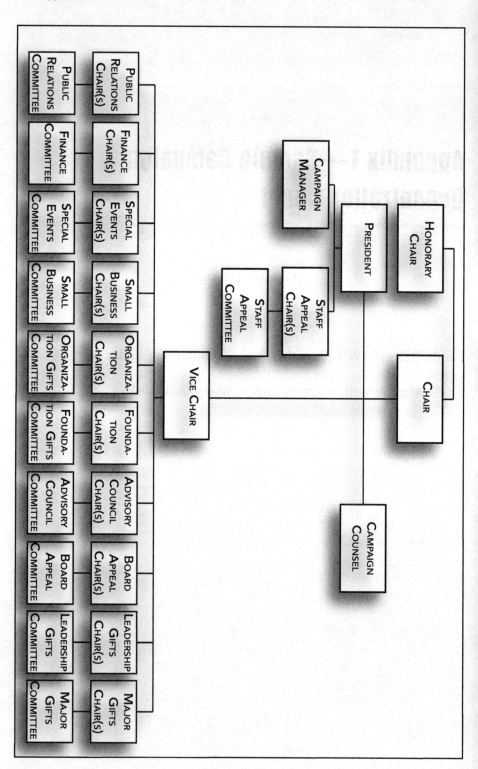

Appendix U—Sample Campaign Budget

[Following pages]

_____

For the full-sized PDF file of this resource contact the author at:

 http://charitychannel.com/cc/linda-lysakowski

Sample Campaign Budget

Item	Month 1	Month 2	Month 3	Month 4	Month 5	Month 6	Month 7	Month 8	Month 9	Month 10	Month 11	Month 12
Consulting Fees	8,000	8,000	8,000	8,000	8,000	8,000	8,000	8,000	8,000	8,000	8,000	8,000
Consulting Expenses	800	800	800	800	800	800	800	800	800	800	800	800
Campaign Assistant-Salary & Taxes	2,000	2,000	2,000	2,000	2,000	2,000	2,000	2,000	2,000	2,000	2,000	2,000
Postage	100	100	100	100	100	100	100	100	100	100	100	100
Staff/Volunteer Travel	100	100	100	100	100	100	100	100	100	100	100	100
Volunteer Meeting Refreshments	100	100	100	100	100	100	100	100	100	100	100	100
Materials: Letterhead/Envelopes	2,000											
Volunteer Training Materials		300		300		300		300		300		300
Materials: Case Statements							2,000					
Materials: Video												
Materials: Brochures												
Materials: Pledge Cards												
Materials: Fact Sheets												
Plaques & Mementos						5,000						
Kick Off Event							2,000					
Phonathon									500			
Direct Mail-Follow Up									300	500		
Ground Breaking												
Monthly Totals	9,300	8,600	17,300	16,000	7,300	12,600	9,300	7,600	8,400	7,800	7,300	7,300

Sample Campaign Budget

Item	Month 13	Month 14	Month 15	Month 16	Month 17	Month 18	Month 19	Month 20	Month 21	Month 22	Month 23	Month 24
Consulting Fees	8,000	8,000	8,000	8,000	8,000	8,000	8,000	8,000	8,000	8,000	8,000	8,000
Consulting Expenses	800	800	800	800	800	800	800	800	800	800	800	800
Campaign Assistant-Salary & Taxes	2,000	2,000	2,000	2,000	2,000	2,000	2,000	2,000	2,000	2,000	2,000	2,000
Postage	100	100	100	100	100	100	100	100	100	100	100	100
Staff/Volunteer Travel	100	100	100	100	100	100	100	100	100	100	100	100
Volunteer Meeting Refreshments	100	100	100	100	100	100	100	100	100	100	100	100
Materials: Letterhead/Envelopes												
Volunteer Training Materials		300		300		300		300				
Materials: Case Statements												
Materials: Video			20,000									
Materials: Brochures			10,000									
Materials: Pledge Cards			500									
Materials: Fact Sheets			500									
Plaques & Mementos						20,000						
Kick Off Event					5,000							
Phonathon									1,000			
Direct Mail-Follow Up									300			
Dedication Event												3,000
Monthly Totals	9,300	8,600	17,300	16,000	7,300	12,600	9,300	7,600	8,400	7,800	7,300	7,300

Budget Total

337,000

Appendix V—Sample Brainstorming Form to Identify New Donors

Potential Donors for our Organization

Your Name:_____

Category	Name & Address	Potential Major Donor Y or N	I will contact this person Y or N
My accountant			
My car dealer			
My banker(s)			
My attorney			
Members of my professional association			

My insurance agent			
My doctor(s)			
My dentist(s)			
Members of a service club to which I belong			
Neighbors			
Relatives			
My clients/ customers			
Politicians I know			
People with whom I worship			
People with whom I work			
People with whom I went to school			
Parents of children with whom my children go to school			
My realtor			
People with whom I do business			
People with whom I play sports			

People I know support other charities			
People who have asked me to support their favorite charity			
People I know who volunteer for other nonprofit organizations			
Others			

For the full-sized PDF file of this resource contact the author at:

 http://charitychannel.com/cc/linda-lysakowski

Appendix W—Sample Confidential Prospect Screening Form

[Following page]

For the full-sized PDF file of this resource contact the author at:

 http://charitychannel.com/cc/linda-lysakowski

Sample Confidential Prospect Screening Form

RATING OF ABILITY	LINKAGES	INTEREST CODES
A. $100,000+	I. Primary contact relationship	1. Active interest in organization
B. 50,000+	II. Alternate contacts relationship	2. Limited interest in organization
C. 25,000+		3. No interest in organization
D. 10,000+		
E. 1,000+		

Screener: _____

Prospect(s) Name	Rating	Interest	Linkage	Suggested Solicitor	Other Pertinent Information

Appendix X—Sample Naming Opportunities for a Theatre

Project	Gift Amount
NAME ON THE BUILDING	$1,000,000
MULTIPURPOSE ROOM	350,000
THEATER	270,000
NEW CAMPUS GATEWAY	250,000
ENTRANCE and LOBBY	150,000
BAND ROOM	150,000
KITCHEN	100,000
KITCHEN EQUIPMENT	75,000
LIGHTING/SOUND FOR THEATER	50,000
MUSIC KEYBOARD ROOM	50,000
MULTIPURPOSE ROOM FURNISHINGS	50,000
THEATER STAGING	50,000
BAND ROOM FURNISHINGS	50,000
SNACK BAR	40,000
FACULTY OFFICES	2 @ 25,000

Project	Gift Amount
THEATER DRESSING ROOMS	2 @ 25,000
MUSIC PRACTICE ROOMS	3 @15,000

For the full-sized PDF file of this resource contact the author at:

 http://charitychannel.com/cc/linda-lysakowski

Appendix Y—Sample Naming Opportunities for Community Center

Room or Facility	# Available	Giving Level	Status
New Addition (may be shared by several donors)	1	$100,000	$60,900 taken
Gym	1	$25,000	half taken/ shared
Bowling Alleys (may be split into 2 @ $7,500)	1	$15,000	1 Taken
Weight Room	1	$10,000	Taken

Men's' Locker Room	1	$10,000	
Ladies' Locker Room	1	$10,000	
Meeting Room	1	$10,000	Taken
Game Room	1	$6,000	Taken
Office	1	$6,000	
Gym Entrance Foyer	1	$6,000	Taken
Computer Station	1	$3,000	Taken
Main Entrance Hallway	1	$3,000	Taken
TV Room	1	$3,000	Taken
Kitchen	1	$3,000	Taken
Storage Area	1	$3,000	

Donors of named gifts will have plaques with their names placed in the area named.

For the full-sized PDF file of this resource contact the author at:

 http://charitychannel.com/cc/linda-lysakowski

Appendix Z—Sample Naming Opportunities for a Life Sciences Center

To Name the Complex	Subject to discussion and approval
Courtyard (2) (ea.)	$500,000
Animal Quarters	500,000
Large (300 Seat) Auditorium	500,000
Small (150) Auditorium	300,000
Classroom Lobby	250,000
Pharmacy Lobby	250,000
Entranceways (2) (ea.)	100,000
Elevators (2) (ea.)	50,000
To Name the First Floor	**1,000,000**
Student Affairs Suite	200,000
Associate Dean for Student Affairs' Office	75,000
Reception & Awards Area	50,000
Student Services Conference Room	25,000
Pre-Professional Advisor's Office	10,000

Undergraduate Laboratories:	
Professional Practice Simulation Laboratory	500,000
Simulation Laboratory	200,000
Drug Information Center	100,000
Computer Simulation Room	100,000
Dispensing Laboratory	100,000
Round Table Demonstration Area	50,000
Recitation Rooms (2) (ea.)	50,000
Office/Workstation	50,000
Taping Rooms (3) (ea.)	25,000
Pharmacy Technology Laboratory	250,000
Manufacturing & Drug Development Laboratory	200,000
Sterile Products Laboratory	100,000
Pharmacy Resource Center	150,000
Organization Rooms (3) (ea.)	25,000
Pharmacy-Toxicology Laboratory	100,000
Toxicology-Drug Metabolism Laboratory	75,000
Department of Pharmacy Practice Suite	150,000
Chairman's Office	75,000
Assistant Dean for Academic Affairs' Office	75,000
Clinical Faculty Office & Workstation Suite I	100,000
Clinical Faculty workstations (4) (ea.)	25,000
Clinical Faculty Offices (9) (ea.)	10,000
Clinical Faculty Office & Workstation Suite II	100,000
Wet Laboratory	75,000
Workstation	25,000
Clinical Faculty Offices (3) (ea.)	10,000
To Name the Second Floor	750,000

Dean's Suite	250,000
Dean's Office	150,000
Reception Area	75,000
Associate Dean for Administrative Affairs' Office	50,000
Pharmacy Development Officer's Office	50,000
Undergraduate Laboratories:	
Pharmacy-Toxicology Laboratory	100,000
Toxicology-Drug Metabolism Laboratory	75,000
Department of Pharmacology Suite	125,000
Chairman's Office	75,000
Center for Applied Pharmacology Office	25,000
Director of Pharmacy Alumni Relations Office	25,000
Pharmacology Research Laboratory Suite I	100,000
Wet Laboratory	75,000
Workstations (2) (ea.)	25,000
Faculty Office	10,000
Pharmacology Research Laboratory Suite II	100,000
Wet Laboratory	75,000
Workstation	25,000
Faculty Offices (2) (ea.)	10,000
Pharmacy Administration Dry Laboratory Suite	100,000
Student Laboratory	75,000
Offices (3)	10,000
Pharmaceutics Wet Laboratory Suite	150,000
Large Wet Laboratory	100,000
Large Workstation	50,000
Offices (2)	10,000
CRYO Storage Laboratory	25,000
Cold Room-Tissue Culture Laboratory	25,000

Department of Medicinal and Biological Chemistry Suite	125,000
Chairman's Office	75,000
Center for Drug Design and Development Office	25,000
Medicinal Chemistry Research Laboratories (8) (ea.)	100,000
Workstations (16) (ea.)	25,000
Faculty Offices (8) (ea.)	10,000
Equipment Suite I	20,000
Equipment Suite II and III (ea.)	10,000
To Name the Third and Fourth Floors (ea.)	750,000
Plant Science Laboratories/Greenhouse Complex	500,000
Greenhouse	300,000
Plant Science Laboratories (2) (ea.)	100,000
Seed Storage	25,000
Records Storage	10,000
Inorganic Chemistry	150,000
Laboratory	75,000
Equipment Room	50,000
Analytical Chemistry	150,000
Laboratories (3) (ea.)	75,000
Physical Chemistry	150,000
Laboratories (2)	75,000
Instrument Room	75,000
Theoretical Chemistry	75,000
Laboratory	75,000
Shared Facilities — Computer Room	50,000
Biochemistry	300,000
Laboratories (2) (ea.)	150,000
Equipment Room	50,000

Cold Laboratory	50,000
Environmental Room	50,000
Developmental Biology Laboratories (2) (ea.)	50,000

For the full-sized PDF file of this resource contact the author at:

 http://charitychannel.com/cc/linda-lysakowski

Glossary

Annual giving: a fundraising program that generates gift support on an annual basis.

Anonymous gift: a gift not publicly attributed to the donor.

Appeal letter: a letter requesting a donation to a fundraising campaign.

Association of Fundraising Professionals (AFP): a professional society (headquartered in Arlington, VA.) that fosters the development and growth of fundraising professionals, works to advance philanthropy and volunteerism and promotes high ethical standards in the fundraising profession. (Formerly, the National Society of Fundraising Executives.)

Bricks and mortar campaign: a capital campaign to meet the financial needs for constructing a physical plant, including facilities and furnishings.

Campaign cabinet: a group, including the chairperson of a capital campaign, that, together with committee chairs, determines campaign policy, and monitors campaign progress.

Capital campaign: an intensive fundraising effort to meet a specific financial goal within a specified period of time for one or more major projects that are out of the ordinary, such as the construction of a facility, the purchase of equipment, or the acquisition of endowment funds.

Case: the reasons why an organization both needs and merits philanthropic support, usually by outlining the organization's programs, current needs, and plans.

Case statement: a presentation that sets forth a case.

CharityChannel: the professional home of tens of thousands of nonprofit-sector colleagues to engage in discussions, contribute articles, collaborate with each other, give and receive training, write books for CharityChannel Press, and attend conferences. http://charitychannel.com.

Chief development officer (CDO): the highest-ranking development staff member responsible for a development program.

Chief executive officer (CEO): the highest-ranking executive responsible for organizational operations.

Cultivation event: a special event (such as a dinner or similar event) to enhance interest in and enthusiasm for the work of an organization.

Database: indexed information held in computer storage from which a computer user can summon selected material. In a database, information is organized so that various programs can access and update data.

Deferred gift: a gift (such as a bequest, life insurance policy, charitable remainder trust, gift annuity, or pooled-income fund) that is committed to a charitable organization, but is not available for use until some future time, usually the death of the donor.

Development audit: an objective evaluation, sometimes conducted by a professional fundraising consultant, of an organization's internal development procedures and results.

Development committee: a group of volunteers responsible for providing leadership, supervision and oversight of an organization's fundraising program.

Development office: the department or division of an organization responsible for all facets of its development program.

Director of Development (DOD): an individual who manages the development programs of an organization.

Donor Bill of Rights: the statement of rights provided a donor.

Endowment: a permanently restricted net asset, the principal of which is protected and the income from which may be spent and is controlled by either the donor's restrictions or the organization's governing board.

Executive Director: an individual who manages or directs an organization's affairs.

Fact sheet: a brief statement of an organization's purposes, programs, services, needs, plans, and other pertinent information prepared in summary form for use by volunteers involved in a campaign.

Feasibility study (see Planning study): an objective survey, usually conducted by a fundraising consultant, of an organization's fundraising potential. The study assesses the strength of the organization's case and the availability of its leaders, workers, and prospective donors. The written report includes the study findings, conclusions, and recommendations.

Gift-acceptance policy: the rules and regulations developed by an organization to determine which types of gifts should or should not be accepted.

Grant: a financial donation given to support a person, organization, project, or program. Most grants are awarded to nonprofit organizations.

Honorary Chair: a person of prominence or influence who agrees to lend his or her name to a campaign.

L-A-I (linkage, ability, interest): the three factors, when considered together, that are indicators of the likelihood of success when soliciting a major gift. Linkage is the association with an organization or constituency; ability is the capacity for giving; interest is the concern about the cause, need, or project.

Leadership gift: a gift, donated at the beginning of a campaign that is expected to set a standard for future giving.

Letter of intent: a declaration stating a person's intention to make a gift or bequest. In some states such a letter constitutes a legal obligation.

Major gift: a significant donation to a nonprofit organization, the amount required to qualify as a major gift being determined by the organization.

Matching gift: a gift by a corporation matching a gift contributed by one or more of its employees.

Memorial gift: a gift in commemoration of a deceased individual.

Mission statement: a statement about a societal need or value that an organization proposes to address.

Philanthropy: love of humankind, usually expressed by an effort to enhance the well-being of humanity through personal acts of practical kindness or by financial support of a cause or causes, such as a charity, mutual aid, or assistance (service clubs, youth groups), quality of life (arts, education, environment), and religion.

Phonathon: a telephone solicitation campaign.

Planning study (see Feasibility study): a fundraising study that places emphasis upon the development of a plan to implement a campaign.

Pledge: a promise that is written, signed, and dated, to fulfill a commitment at some future time; specifically, a financial promise payable according to terms agreed to by the donor. Such pledges may be legally enforceable, subject to state law.

Pledge card: a printed form used by a donor as a response to an appeal.

Pledge payment: payment of all or a portion of a pledge.

Press release: an official statement (such as a story, item, or other announcement) issued to newspapers for publication.

Prospect: any potential donor whose linkages, giving ability, and interests have been confirmed.

Prospect research: the continuing search for pertinent information on prospects and donors.

Prospect screening: a preliminary evaluation of broad categories of potential donors prior to rating.

Request for proposal (RFP): an announcement issued by an organization seeking delivery of goods or services according to specifications.

Response device: a form or envelope used for conveying a reply to a mailed appeal.

Role-playing: in fundraising, coaching volunteers by having them perform the roles of solicitor and prospect in preparation for an actual solicitation.

Special event: a function designed to attract and involve people in an organization or cause.

Steering Committee: a committee of top volunteer leaders who oversee and manage a campaign or other fundraising effort.

Stewardship: a process whereby an organization seeks to be worthy of continued philanthropic support, including the acknowledgment of gifts, donor recognition, the honoring of donor intent, prudent investment of gifts, and the effective and efficient use of funds to further the mission of the organization.

Strategic plan: decisions and actions that shape and guide an organization while emphasizing the future implications of present decisions. This plan usually employs the SWOT analysis.

Suspect: a possible source of support whose philanthropic interests appear to match those of a particular organization, but whose linkages, giving ability, and interests have not yet been confirmed.

Unrestricted gift: a gift made without any condition or designation.

Vision statement: a statement about what an organization can and should become at some future time.

Adapted with permission from the Association of Fundraising Professionals (AFP) Dictionary of Fundraising Terms

Index

FUNDRAI$ING
as a Career

What, Are You Crazy?

www.charitychannel.com

*Charity*Channel
PRESS

50 A$KS
in 50 Weeks

A Guide to Better Fundraising for
Your Small Development Shop

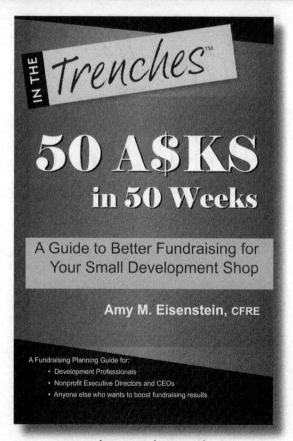

www.charitychannel.com

PRESS

ASKING
about Asking
Mastering the Art of Conversational Fundraising™

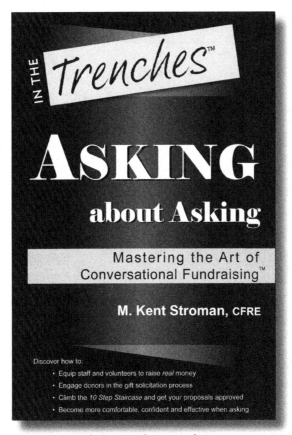

IN THE *Trenches*™

ASKING
about Asking

Mastering the Art of Conversational Fundraising™

M. Kent Stroman, CFRE

Discover how to:
- Equip staff and volunteers to raise *real* money
- Engage donors in the gift solicitation process
- Climb the *10 Step Staircase* and get your proposals approved
- Become more comfortable, confident and effective when asking

www.charitychannel.com

*Charity*Channel
PRESS™

Just Released!

YOU AND YOUR
Nonprofit

Practical Advice and Tips from the
CharityChannel Professional Community

www.charitychannel.com

PRESS

CPSIA information can be obtained
at www.ICGtesting.com
Printed in the USA
FSOW04n0213251215
14588FS